Galatians

BREAKAWAY TO FREEDOM

HEART
STEALERS
BIBLE STUDIES

A scriptual guide
for today's woman

Sarah L. Howell

God's Word to you is our highest calling.

Heart Stealers Bible Studies
Galatians: Breakaway to Freedom

First Printing, 2006

ISBN: 0-89957-104-2

Cover design by ImageWright Marketing and Design, Chattanooga, TN

Interior design and typesetting by PerfecType, Nashville, TN

Editing by Rick Steele

Proofreading by Christy Graeber

Printed in Canada

10 09 08 07 06 05 –T– 6 5 4 3 2 1

This book is dedicated to Sonny Howell, Michele Shively, Shannon Cartrett, and all the women of Community Lighthouse Bible Study. Thank you for believing in me.

ACKNOWLEDGMENTS

I am so thankful for Jennifer Mulvany, Kim Cook, Krystee Edwards, Carly Abbott, Natalie Adams, Lauren Newman, Lindsay Pracht, Hayley Pharr, and Ashley Smith. Thank you ladies for your edits and for your willingness to critique this study. You women are amazing!

I'm not sure if most writers like their editors, but I feel so blessed to have mine. Rick Steele, you have believed in this study from its inception. Thank you for your vision and for your instruction during this entire process. Kudos also go to Christy Graeber for your excellent proofreading.

Lauren, Abby, and Leah, thank you for limiting your requests for mommy to get off the computer to only fifteen a day. Thank you for sustaining yourselves on a diet of cheese crackers and goldfish while mommy stared at the blinking cursor and suffered from writer's block. And above all, thank you for your distracting smiles and impromptu hugs that took my mind off the task at hand and allowed me to enjoy life. I love you girls!

I am so blessed to have my parents, Darryl and Marcie Akiona, and my in-laws, Charles and Jayne Howell. Thank you for your unconditional love and acceptance. And thank you for giving me the freedom to be the woman God created me to be. I dearly love you all.

A special thanks to my pastors, Brad and Jennifer Evangelista. Thank you for your friendship. And thank you that the pursuit of your vision for CrossPointe Church has inspired me to pursue my own vision. Faith, hope, and love to you both.

And finally, to my Abba Daddy, who told me, "Do not be afraid . . . and write." Thank you for your gentle prodding. Thank you for the way you opened your Word to me in a new way. And thank you for allowing me to steal your heart, because you've certainly stolen mine. I love you.

ABOUT THE AUTHOR

Sarah L. Howell has a special calling to serve women. She has led small-group Bible studies in Phoenix, Arizona, and in Atlanta, Georgia. Her passion for God's Word that was sparked through these studies ignited her pursuit to eventually teach God's Word and write Bible study curriculum. Sarah has a bachelor's degree from Lee University. While studying at Lee and foundering in her dating life, Sarah become enamored with Song of Solomon 4:9, "You have stolen my heart, my sister, my bride; you have stolen my heart with one glance of your eyes." It was through this scripture that she realized for the first time that she was a "heart stealer." Knowing that she had stolen her Savior's heart changed her life forever. This verse has inspired her to write books for women in the Heart Stealers Bible Studies series for AMG Publishers.

In 1995, Sarah was caught stealing again. This time, she stole the heart of her husband, Sonny Howell. Over the past ten years of their marriage, they have ministered to youth, young couples, and young adults in Tennessee, Arizona, and Georgia. Currently, Sarah and her husband reside in Columbus, Georgia, with their three young daughters: Lauren, Abby, and Leah. They serve on staff at CrossPointe Church in Fortson, Georgia, where Sarah is actively involved in the women's ministry. For more information concerning Sarah and the Heart Stealers line of Bible studies, log on to:

www.heartstealers.com

CONTENTS

About the Study *xiii*

Introduction: The Faith to Breakaway 1

Breakaway from Others' Opinions 9

Breakaway from the Ordinary 35

Breakaway from Doubt 63

Breakaway from Legalism 89

Breakaway to Freedom 115

Breakaway to Love 139

ABOUT THE STUDY

If you're like me, then you probably skip right over this part. But on the off chance you're not like me and are much more attentive to detail, then I want you to know I'm writing this section especially for you. So thanks for taking the time to read it!

If you're embarking upon this spiritual breakaway with others by your side, then the questions with a heart by them are intended for discussion within your small group. However, if you are like the apostle Paul and your flight to freedom is a solo journey, then please feel free to answer the discussion questions with unfettered honesty. (Because no one except you and God will know your answers!)

In addition to the discussion questions, each lesson contains a specific verse from the passage of study that best depicts the theme for the week. This verse is known as the V.O.W. or the **Verse of the Week.** If you're feeling especially studious, then please feel free to commit this verse to memory. But if your scholastic energy has already been exhausted for the week, then just enjoy the scripture.

The **Interact with Your iPod** section is for all you music fans out there. I wish I could say I was cool enough to actually own an iPod, but I'm not. I download my music the old fashioned way–on the computer. (Legally, I might add!) At any rate, the **Interact with Your iPod** sections are strictly optional. You can complete the study without downloading the music. But personally, I think the music is the best part of the study, because now I can't listen to Kelly Clarkson, U2, Tim McGraw, or Coldplay without thinking of Galatians.

Finally, I've concluded each daily segment of the study with a prayer of my own. These prayers are my honest response to the things God revealed to me during the writing of this study. And initially, I fully intended for those prayers to be the only prayers offered in this book. However, a good friend of mine, Lindsay Pracht, suggested I provide readers with the same opportunity I had–the opportunity to respond to God in prayer. So as a result of Lindsay's suggestion, we've included a prayer journal in the back of this study. Please use it to pen your own prayer to the Father. You can do it on a daily basis as I did, or you can simply do it whenever you feel led to do so. But I encourage you to utilize this portion of the book. Tell God how you feel. Share with him your failures and your triumphs. Let him know your questions and your concerns. Just talk to him in your own way. Because your breakaway to freedom isn't dependent upon a set of rules and regulations; it is dependent upon a relationship with the Father. And prayer is the foundation upon which that relationship is built. So write away!!

THE FAITH TO BREAKAWAY

Introduction to Galatians

VOW (Verse of the Week): "What is more, I consider everything a loss compared to the surpassing greatness of knowing Christ Jesus my Lord, for whose sake I have lost all things. I consider them rubbish, that I may gain Christ and be found in him, not having a righteousness of my own that comes from the law, but that which is through faith in Christ."	Philippians 3:8, 9

It would have been easy to stay in her small town, watching the rain fall from the back seat of her parents' car. But the red carpet visions with the cameras flashing and the intoxicating allure of fame and popularity were too persistent. They called to the young eight-year-old, whose nightly ritual was a bedside prayer for the strength to spread her wings, to take a risk and a chance, and finally to . . . breakaway.

Kelly Clarkson's 2004 video for her number one single, "Breakaway," was in reality a synopsis of her life. While her nightly prayers may not have been quite as poetic, the scenes portrayed in the video were based on real-life experiences–her first fearful airplane flight, Texas thunderstorms, and her job as a theater attendant.

Look up the following verses and record the life experiences of the apostle Paul (also referred to as Saul).

Acts 22:2, 3

___

___

___

Acts 22:4

___

___

___

Acts 22:6–8

___

___

___

Acts 22:12–16

___

___

___

Kelly Clarkson's life story embodied the theme of her song. And somehow, it made the song's message more powerful. The apostle Paul, author of Galatians, was once known to be a devout Jew whose commitment to the law and Judaism was unwavering. He clung to Judaic law and allowed it to dictate his life–until God called him to breakaway.

Breaking away for Paul did not require leaving the small town of Burleson, Texas, to enter a twenty-first century talent show. For him, it required something far greater. Paul's breakaway meant abandoning the rules and regulations in which he'd found solace. It meant admitting he'd been wrong about Christ and Christianity. It meant a loss of social status. It meant expulsion from the synagogue. It meant enduring the betrayal of friends and the hatred of others. But most of all, Paul's breakaway meant freedom–freedom from the routine of religion, freedom to go full force after God.

The book of Galatians is about freedom, and it was written by an author whose life exemplified the message he wrote. Although Paul was once immersed in the regulations of legalism, he found true freedom when he encountered Jesus Christ. His breakaway from the familiar to set out in pursuit of Christ became the theme of his life.

Read Philippians 3:8, 9. What is Paul passionate about in these verses?

____

____

____

____

____

Paul's passion for the Lord caused him to forsake the confines of the law and walk by faith in Christ. His faith walk led him to do amazing things for the cause of Christ, one of which was to author the book of Galatians. At the time Galatians was written, Paul was enjoying his newfound freedom in Christ and living in Syrian Antioch. He wrote his liberating message around AD 48 to four churches (possibly more) in the Roman province of Galatia. These churches, which had been founded during Paul's first missionary journey, consisted of both Jewish and Gentile (non-Jews) believers.

Kelly Clarkson's "Breakaway" video makes the audience privy to flashbacks of her childhood. In the book of Acts, the Bible offers us the same opportunity to take a look back into the Galatians' early stages of development. In Acts, we see Paul's entrance into the province of Galatia during his first missionary journey around AD 46. The first town he settled in was Pisidian Antioch. It would later be one of the four churches Paul addressed in the book of Galatians.

Upon their initial entrance into this city, Paul and his sidekick Barnabas entered the Jewish synagogue and addressed the Jews and Gentiles. Paul told them of Christ's death, burial, and resurrection. He reminded them of the Old Testament prophecies that foretold the coming of the Messiah. And he informed them that as a result of Christ's work on earth, salvation was available for all mankind.

Read Acts 13:42–44 and record how the people responded to the gospel message.

At first, it seems as though the people in Pisidian Antioch were eager to embrace a gospel based upon faith in Christ. They were anxious to hear more from Paul and Barnabas about this message that liberated them from the law. However, as time progressed, it became evident that not everyone felt the same way.

Read Acts 13:45, 46, 50, 51.

Who rejected the gospel?

What did these people do to Paul and Barnabas?

What did Paul and Barnabas do in response to their rejection?

Propelled onward by his passion for Christ, Paul made a second stop in the province of Galatia and arrived in the town of Iconium. This city also contained a Jewish synagogue, and Paul made that his venue to preach the gospel. At first the combined congregation of Jews and Gentiles eagerly accepted the truth. But, as in Pisidian Antioch, there were some Jews who refused to believe.

Read Acts 14:1–7.

What controversy is described in verses 4 and 5?

According to verses 6 and 7, what was the outcome?

At this point, it seems as though Paul is fighting a losing battle. However, the need for the book of Galatians, written two years after his visits, is proof that his missionary efforts during this first journey to Galatia are not in vain. Somewhere along the way, despite assassination plots and city riots, Paul's gospel of freedom found residence in the hearts of a handful of believers.

Thanks to the believers in Lystra, Paul persisted in his missionary effort despite the rejection and persecution that surrounded him. When Paul arrived in Lystra to inform the citizens of Christ's liberating gospel, he stumbled upon a lame man and instructed the man to stand to his feet. The man obeyed Paul and was healed (Acts 14:8–10).

This proved to be a rather controversial miracle. Read Acts 14:11–13. How did the crowd respond to this miracle?

After being booted out of two cities, Paul finally finds a little love in Lystra. Though the crowd's admiration of him took the form of idolatry, at least he and Barnabas were well received. I wonder if Paul's warm reception caused him to feel the same way Kelly Clarkson felt when she won *American Idol* and became the object of worship for every small town girl with big hopes and dreams.

Read Acts 14:14, 15 and record how Paul felt.

____

____

____

Well, no delusions of grandeur in those verses. No pursuit of personal success for Paul; just an all-out passion to bring the good news of freedom to everyone. The citizens of Lystra obviously got the point, because they stopped worshiping Paul and Barnabas immediately.

Read Acts 14:19, 20 and record what happens next.

____

____

____

____

Just when things are looking up, some Jews from Antioch and Iconium railroad Paul. And in keeping with tradition, Paul is rather violently expelled from town. (I think at this point, he's 0 for 3.) But, undaunted by his near-death experience, Paul continues on to the Galatian city of Derbe. Here, he preaches the good news and actually wins over a large number of disciples (see Acts 14:21).

Amid seeming defeat and rejection, Paul managed to remain a free spirit, breaking away from the traditions and legalisms of his past, and courageously journeying onward to ensure others the opportunity to hear his gospel message. His passion inspires me and causes me to wonder what his song of freedom would have sounded like had he sung a pop rock song like Kelly Clarkson's.

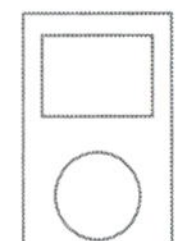

Interact with Your iPod®

Download Kelly Clarkson's "Breakaway" and ask yourself how Paul would have felt had he heard Clarkson's song.

- Would he have sung it on his journeys from Pisidian Antioch, Iconium, Lystra, and Derbe?
- Does her song inspire you to breakaway from the routine of Christianity and, like Paul, go full force for God?

Paul's passion for Christ enabled him to breakaway in spite of personal hardships and difficulties. Cite a time in your life when you were so passionate about something you were willing to breakaway and go after it despite adversity.

____

____

____

Prayer—*Lord, thank you for Paul's example of courage and passion. God, I want to be a woman of passion; a woman who breaks away from the routine of religion and goes after you full force. Give me the courage and faith to pursue only you and to follow you on your journey for my life.*

BREAKAWAY FROM OTHERS' OPINIONS

Galatians Chapter 1

VOW (Verse Of the Week): "Am I now trying to win the approval of men, or of God? Or am I trying to please men? If I were still trying to please men, I would not be a servant of Christ."	**Galatians 1:10**

Day 1: A Life God "MEST" with

Read Galatians 1:1.

In the Blue Island section of the south side of Chicago, cousins Tony and Matt Lovato grew up sharing a love for music. Beginning their musical debut at age seven with borrowed instruments, Tony and Matt honed their talents with aspirations of playing in a punk rock band. In the mid 1990s, to further their dream, they added a guitarist, Jeremiah Rangel, and a drummer, Nick Gigler, to their musical group. Their band began playing in local Chicago punk clubs and gradually garnered a following.

Their fan base grew even larger after the July 2000 release of their first major label debut, *Wasting Time,* from Maverick Records. They further expanded their following with the release of their second album, *Destination Unknown,* in 2001. To promote their CD, they traveled nationwide on a non-stop tour, playing in various venues for nearly two years. This grassroots effort won them a substantial fan base.

From your introductory lesson, what cities in Galatia did the apostle Paul tour in order to promote his message?

____

____

What kind of fan base did he garner? Did it consist of Jews and Gentiles?

____

____

What was his expulsion rate from these four cities?

____

____

Much like Tony and Matt Lovato's Chicago-based band, Paul also set out on a grassroots effort to promote his message among Jews and Gentiles with a tour most theologians refer to as "Paul's First Missionary Journey." However, Paul's proclivity for inciting the anger of others created controversy that would have put any punk rock band to shame. His divisive message definitely pushed the envelope. The same could be said for the explicit lyrics, multiple tattoos, and body piercing of Lovato's band. But while such antics from an alternative band in the twenty-first century result in a fan base, Paul's efforts resulted in multiple expulsions.

Read Galatians 1:1. Despite his constant rejection, how did Paul identify himself?

____

____

Read Acts 9:4–19 and Acts 13:1–3. What significant events occurred in Paul's (a.k.a. Saul) life to shape his identity and assure him of his calling?

____

____

When Tony and Matt Lovato went in search of a name to identify their band, their journey didn't take them very far. In fact, it took them as far as the fridge, where they found a case of Milwaukee's Best Beer. Upon the sight of their favorite drink, inspiration came and Tony suggested the name of their band be "Mest"–a spoonerism of the words "Milwaukee's Best" (Bilwaukee's Mest). With a rather intoxicating identity, Mest has gained popularity in the United States and abroad.

Read Philippians 3:4–6. Prior to his conversion, what did Paul get his identity from?

____

____

Fortunately, it wasn't a case of beer. No, prior to his salvation, Paul's identity came from something far more lethal; it came from the toxin of pride. Paul's former drug of choice, his selfish pride, was based upon his Jewish heritage and his Jewish accomplishments. At the time he wrote Philippians, he had overcome his addiction to self and found his identity in Christ. His writings in Philippians are an attempt to warn the Philippians not to put their confidence and identity in themselves, but rather to pursue an identity based on Christ.

His reference to himself in Galatians 1:1 reveals a man who had found his identity in God alone, not in his worldly accomplishments, nor in the rejection he had encountered at the hands of men.

How do you think Paul got to this point in his life?

Understand that when Paul wrote the book of Galatians, there were people in the Galatian churches who were questioning Paul's apostleship. They were belittling his teachings and undermining his authority. Yet, despite their opinions of him, he remained resolute in his identity and in his calling.

Such confidence and sheer determination can only be manifested in someone whom God has *mest* with. God definitely *mest* with Paul on the road to Damascus. God *mest* with Paul's ideas, with his thoughts, with his future, and even with Paul's own views of himself. And I believe the secret to Paul's victory over selfish pride is that Paul chose to believe everything God thought about him.

The following verses in Ephesians list the things Paul believed about what God thought of him. Below each scripture reference, write what it says God did for us.

Ephesians 1:3, 4

Ephesians 1:5

____

____

Ephesians 1:11

____

____

In Galatians, Paul identified himself as an apostle called by God. Sure, his Damascus road conversion and his experience at the church in Antioch served to further validate his calling. But deep within his heart, the core values that formed his identity were based upon the premise that Paul believed he was chosen by God to be holy and blameless. He believed God had predestined him to be adopted as his son, and he believed he had been chosen to be a part of God's plan.

I like the first chapter of Ephesians because it's not just a creed of core beliefs for Paul's life; it's a creed of core beliefs for every Christian's life. It reveals to us our true identity in Christ by portraying God's opinion of us, an opinion that deems us chosen, holy and blameless, adopted as God's, and a part of God's plan.

Does God's opinion of you mess with your identity? If so, how?

____

____

____

____

____

____

Prayer–*Lord, I want my life to be a life that you have* mest *with. A life identified by your thoughts and opinions of me. On this earth, where I am surrounded by the critical opinions of others and the lies of the enemy, give me the courage to believe you, and only you.*

Day 2: A Church God "MEST" with

Read Galatians 1:2–5.

In Day One, we received insight into God's view of Paul and how God's opinion determined Paul's view of himself. Today, we will discover God's opinion of the Galatians, but first, let's take a look at Paul's opinion of them.

Read the following passages and answer the questions.

Scripture	**To whom is Paul addressing this letter?**	**Does he use any adjectives to describe his audience? If so, what are they?**
Galatians 1:2		
Ephesians 1:1		
Colossians 1:2		

When the group Mest came to mind as an illustration for this study, I wasn't fond of the idea, mainly because I'm not a Mest fan. For me, it's hard to develop an affinity for a group of wild guys whose vocabulary is replete with four-letter expletives and whose idea of a good time is throwing house parties where the first guest to pass out is disrobed and photographed for future humiliation.[1] As a person who's never been much into nude photography, it's difficult for me to hold a group like Mest in high esteem. I think Paul encountered the same difficulty as he wrote his letter to the Galatians. It wasn't that he didn't love the Galatians; he wouldn't have bothered writing to them if he didn't love them. No, I don't think it was a matter of love. I think it was more a matter of respect.

Read Galatians 3:1 and write the adjective Paul uses to describe the Galatians.

When greeting the Ephesians, Paul describes his audience as faithful saints. When writing his letter to the Colossians, Paul states that these believers were holy and faithful brothers. But when writing to the Galatians, Paul bestows no warm and fuzzy commendations in his salutation. Rather, Paul reserves his opinion of them until the third chapter–an opinion his audience might have preferred he kept to himself.

Read Galatians 1:6, 7. What did the Galatians do to cause Paul to lose respect for them?

---

1. Joe D'Angelo, "Good Charlotte's Benji Helps Mest Get 'Jaded,'" *MTV News,* May 22, 2003, http://www.vh1.com/news/articles/1472008/05212003/mest.jhtml.

Would you have lost respect for them? Describe your reasoning for your answer.

____

____

____

I love the book of Galatians because God allowed Paul to formulate his own opinion. Now, as we'll see in further study, Paul's opinion was not necessarily in alignment with God's opinion, but nonetheless, Paul was given opportunity to voice his feelings and thoughts.

Read Galatians 1:3–5 to discover God's opinion of the Galatians. In verse three, what two things are bestowed upon them from God and Jesus?

____

God the Father and Jesus Christ granted grace and peace to the audience of Paul's letter. Paul deemed the Galatians unwise, but the Father and Son deemed them worthy of grace and peace. The word "grace" in this passage is best described as an unearned gift that unites us with God, while the word "peace" refers to, "peace of mind, tranquility, arising from reconciliation with God."[2]

Despite their attraction to a false gospel, God still thought the Galatians worthy of his grace and peace. Grace was the gift God offered in order to reconcile the Galatians back to him, and peace was the product of that reconciliation. God still wanted to reclaim a right relationship with the Galatians. And he thought them worthy of his love, even if Paul thought them foolish.

2. Spiros Zodhiates, *The Complete Word Study Dictionary* (Chattanooga, TN: AMG Publishers, 1992), 519.

If you were a member of the Galatian church, whose assessment would you choose to believe–Paul's or God's? How would your decision influence your opinion of yourself?

____

____

____

____

____

____

Cite the names of people whose opinions you've allowed to influence your life. Are their opinions of you in alignment with God's opinion of you?

____

____

____

Prayer–*Lord, I admit I'm not perfect. I sin like everyone else, and my sins must seem so foolish in your sight. The worst thing about my sin is not that I commit it, but that it separates me from you. But thank you that in the midst of my folly, you still deem me worthy of your grace and peace. Thank you for never giving up on me, even when others did. Give me the faith to see myself as you see me and to run to you in repentance when my sins have alienated me from you.*

Day 3: "MEST" Up by Others' Opinions

Read Galatians 1:6–10.

In Day Two, we saw how two different descriptions of the Galatian church could have easily identified this body of believers. Today we will see how some distorted opinions nearly destroyed this church.

Read Galatians 1:6, 7.

Remember Paul's description of the Galatians examined in Day Two. Now describe Paul's tone as he writes these verses to the Galatians.

In verse 6, what does Paul accuse the Galatians of doing?

In verse 7, Paul refers to "some people." Theologians refer to this group as Judaizers. What two things were these Judaizers doing?

The Galatians believed a perverted gospel which taught that you had to be circumcised in order to be holy. Read Galatians 5:2–4. According to verse 4, what were the Galatians trying to do?

By believing a perverted gospel and reverting back to the Mosaic Law that required circumcision, the Galatians were in essence binding themselves again to the law from which they had once been freed. They were once again trying to obtain holiness based on their own abilities instead of Christ's abilities. But how did they get to this point? When Paul left them after his visit, they were obviously following the truth. He even refers to their former obedience in Galatians 5:7.

Write Galatians 5:7 below.

____

____

____

To answer Paul's question, read Galatians 1:7–9. What phrase is repeated in these verses?

____

____

To learn of the original message Paul preached to the Galatians, turn to Acts 13:38–39. According to verse 39, what must everyone do in order to be justified?

____

____

In Galatians 1:7–9, Paul bluntly states that no other gospel should be believed except the one that teaches that people are justified (which means "made righteous") through their belief in Christ. Unfortunately, somewhere along the way, the Galatians had been deceived into believing a distorted gospel–one that required certain works and acts in order to be made righteous.

After being freed from the rules and regulations of the law, why do you think the Galatians would go back to it?

In 2001, prior to her first appearance on *American Idol,* Kelly Clarkson broke away from Burleson, Texas, and made her way to Los Angeles to pursue a singing career. Her stint away from home was short-lived, however, because her LA apartment burned down, leaving her homeless. After sleeping in her car for a while, she finally sought solace in the familiar and returned to Burleson.[3]

Just as Clarkson was wooed back home, the Galatians may have been wooed back to legalism because it was familiar to them. They probably didn't return to the familiar as a result of a house fire and subsequent period of homelessness, but nonetheless, they returned to their bondage. I wonder if some people like bondage because it's so predictable and familiar. There's no threat of change with bondage. It is forever the same. But freedom, on the other hand, is fraught with unpredictability.

Perhaps familiarity was one reason the Galatians returned to their bondage, but Paul offers another reason in Galatians 1:10. He clothes his diagnosis in the form of a question about himself, but if we look closely, we can see how this character flaw could have easily caused the Galatians to abandon the truth of Christ.

Read Galatians 1:10 and write the character flaw Paul refers to in this passage.

---

3. Hunter Haulk, "Clarkson Still in the Spotlight," *Quick,* May 10, 2005, http://www.quickdfw.com/home/poplife/stories/quick0510kelly.915e0e29.html.

On November 13, 2001, Mest released its sophomore album, *Destination Unknown.* The song, "Cadillac" gained the most exposure, while a lesser-known title, "Opinions," quietly became a fan favorite. Written by lead singer Tony Lovato, "Opinions" addresses the dilemma of pleasing people by listening to their opinions.

Lovato's lyrics give some really good insight into the life of a person torn between the opinions of others. In his opening verse he explains how he's frustrated by his attempts to please others. He questions the futility of making others happy when his efforts often come at the expense of his own happiness.

After listening to the opinions of others and subsequently falling away from the faith, do you think the Galatians were happy? Why or why not?

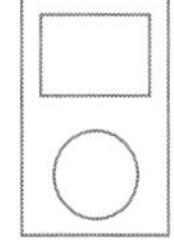

Interact with Your iPod®

Download Mest's punk rock song "Opinions." (I promise this one doesn't have any expletives in it!)

- Do you think this song conveys what the Galatians' state of mind may have been after listening to the opinions of others?
- Does this song convey your state of mind when you're torn between the opinions of others?

> On January 13, 2006, despite fans' opinions that they should remain together, *Mest* announced that they have no intention of performing together in the future. According to their MySpace blog, their current "So Long and Thanx For the Booze Tour" will indeed be their last tour together.[4]

The Galatians had gotten themselves into a state of confusion by listening to the opinions of the Judaizers. In Galatians 1:10, Paul explains why the Galatians were so susceptible to the opinions of others. In his typical direct manner, he diagnoses their problem by using himself as an example. His diagnosis is that the Galatians' desire was to please men.

The Galatians' desire to please people led them to believe a false gospel that subsequently led them to a state of confusion. So often the desire to please people leads to undesirable results. Tony Lovato stated as much in his song, "Opinions."

If the consequence for pleasing others is so great, why do we do it?

____

____

____

____

____

4. Tony Lavato, "Thanx for the Memories . . ." blog.myspace.com, January 13, 2006, http://blog.myspace.com/index.cfm?fuseaction=blog.view&friendID=3011519&blogID=77444885&MyToken=93a558c4-40d4-42b2-954f-14d1eb14b884.

Prayer–*Lord, I am so guilty of this. I don't want to be, but I am. A part of me wants to please you more than anything else in this world, and yet the other part of me is tempted to pursue the approval of others. I want people to like me God, but not at the expense of pleasing you. Please Lord, show me how to pursue your approval alone, because I don't want to be in bondage to pleasing others. Help me in this area, because I cannot do it by myself.*

Day 4: Breakaway from Others' Opinions

Read Galatians 1:11–17.

Paul wrote the next few verses we will study in Galatians as a defense of the gospel. He wrote this passage to persuade the Galatians that his message was indeed from God and not based on the opinions of men. As Paul makes his defense, he not only proves his message to be divinely inspired, but he also gives us insight into his own life and how he managed to break away from the opinions of others and please God.

Read Galatians 1:11, 12. Paul makes four points about his message in these verses. Can you find all four points?

____

____

____

It must have been pretty important to Paul to convince his readers that men did not invent the gospel he preached and wrote about. In fact, he states as much in verse 11. Then he continues to argue he'd neither received this gospel from others, nor had he been taught it by others, but rather had received it by revelation from Jesus.

Why do you think it was so important to Paul to convince his readers his message did not originate from the opinions of others?

I'm sure Paul wanted to prove the divine origin of the words he preached, but I also wonder if Paul might have been trying to prove the unreliability of any gospel that originated from men. We all know that people are fallible. But why are they so fallible?

Write Jeremiah 17:9 below.

As humans, we often have a tendency to allow our hearts to dictate our opinions. As Jeremiah teaches us, our hearts can deceive us into believing something that is not in alignment with scripture. Paul's life reflects this deception.

Read Galatians 1:13, 14. This passage records a time in Paul's life when he was deceived by his own heart and by the opinions of others. Describe what Paul did during this time.

Whose opinions (or traditions) was he following?

Read Galatians 1:15, 16. What did God do for Paul, according to these verses?

Thankfully for Paul, God saved him from his own deceptive heart and from the erroneous opinions of his fathers by revealing Christ to him. Verse 15 indicates that God was the initiator of the entire process. First, God set Paul apart from birth. Then God called Paul by his grace, and finally, God revealed his Son through Paul.

God had a purpose for doing all these things. According to verse 16, what is one reason God did all of this for Paul?

In verse 16, what important thing did Paul not do after God touched his life?

God obviously had a big plan for Paul's life, a plan that placed Paul in the role of missionary to the Gentiles. To protect this newly found gospel message and to protect God's plan for his life, Paul refused to allow these precious gifts to be *mest* up by the opinions of men.

What does verse 17 say Paul did after that?

I admire Paul because after hearing from God, he didn't require human validation regarding God's plan for his life or regarding this new gospel. He didn't think it necessary to journey to Jerusalem, even though Jerusalem housed the Jewish temple and was the birthplace of the Christian church on the Day of Pentecost (Acts 2). And for whatever reason, Paul did not seek guidance from the apostles in Jerusalem. Rather he went to Arabia and later to Damascus.

Theologians don't really know why Paul chose Arabia. The book of Acts does not record his journey there; in fact, Paul's mention of Arabia in Galatians is the only reference to his expedition there. I can only speculate why Paul went to Arabia, but this passage is reminiscent of another that recounts how Jesus spent some time in seclusion before beginning his ministry.

Read Mark 1:9–12. After Christ's baptism, which signified his entrance into ministry, what did he do?

____

____

Christ was moved by the Spirit to the desert. While there he was tempted by Satan three times, but since Christ was there forty days, he also had plenty of opportunity to commune with his Father. Surely he had plenty of time to hear the directives and opinions of the one he desired to please.

I believe Paul spent his time in Arabia doing much the same thing, spending time with this God whom he'd always believed in but had never communed with. Arabia was Paul's chance to be alone with God. It was his secret place, his prayer closet, his altar where he met with the Father. And over time, Paul's solitude with the Lord caused him to release his desire to please men and replace it with a desire to please God, and God alone.

Galatians 1:17 tells us that Paul returned to Damascus after his stay in Arabia. Damascus is where Paul first met the Lord. So it is possible that his return to this city reminded him of his initial encounter with Christ. Sometimes, in this world that is ever changing, it's comforting to go back to those moments in our lives where Christ revealed himself to us. Such moments strengthen our faith and encourage us onward in our pursuit to please the one whom we've never seen, but have often encountered.

Like Paul, do you have an Arabia–a place where you seek solitude with God? If so, where is it and how do you feel when you're there?

____

____

____

____

____

____

____

____

Do you have a Damascus–a memory of a time or place when God spoke to you or revealed himself to you in a powerful way? If so, share it below.

____

____

____

Solitude with God is the only thing that will liberate us from our tendency to please others. In seclusion with him, his opinion becomes the only thing that matters, and the opinions of others lose their influence on our lives. Thankfully, Paul sought seclusion with the Father, and as a result, he was freed from his desire to please men. Paul's breakaway from the opinions of others is an encouragement to all who are in pursuit of the Father's heart.

Prayer—*God, I don't want to be bound by my desire to please people. I want to be free to please you, Lord, and you alone. Help me seek moments of solitude with you so that your opinion will take precedence in my life.*

Day 5: The Reward for Pursuing God's Opinion

Read Galatians 1:18–24.

Paul's intent for writing Galatians 1 was to prove to his audience that no one had *mest* with the gospel he preached. It had been divinely inspired and untainted by human beliefs or opinions. His solitude in Arabia had enabled him to listen to the voice of the Lord and ensure that the gospel message he had received was indeed an accurate one. Today we will learn how his confidence in the gospel message and his passion to please the Lord reaped eternal rewards.

Read Acts 22:3.

How does Paul describe himself in this verse?

____

Why do you think God chose to entrust his gospel to Paul?

____

____

Read Galatians 1:18–20. Which important person did Paul visit in Jerusalem?

Read Matthew 16:13–17. What important confession did this disciple make?

According to verse 17, why was he able to make this confession?

The apostle Paul was a student of the Old Testament. He had studied the law and the prophets since his boyhood. As a Pharisee, he had dedicated his life to the study of the Word of God. However, despite all this knowledge, he did not recognize Jesus as the Messiah until God revealed this to him on the road to Damascus.

Peter's revelation of Jesus as the Messiah was similar in that God also revealed it to him. After revealing this message to Peter, Christ placed a mantle of authority on him and identified his faith as a foundational faith that would enable Christ's church to be built. Three years after his conversion, Paul decided to visit this instrumental leader of the New Testament church.

While the two must have discussed spiritual matters, Paul indicates the purpose of his visit was merely to get acquainted with Peter.

He did not receive the gospel message from Peter, nor did he seek Peter's opinion of his gospel. Prior to his conversion, Peter was a fisherman by trade. Because Peter was a devout Jew, he was familiar with the basic laws of Judaism and the Old Testament. But Peter had not studied the Old Testament as Paul had. Paul had a foundation in the Word, and when God revealed Christ to him, Paul was able to understand how the law and the prophets of the Old Testament foreshadow the coming of Christ.

It was Paul's confidence in the Word and his freedom from the opinions of men that enabled him to put so much faith in God. He needed neither Peter's nor the apostles' validation of his message. His gospel had been given and validated by the only one whose opinion really mattered.

Read Galatians 1:21. After his short visit in Jerusalem, where did Paul go?

Paul makes a point of reminding his audience that he did not remain in the city of Jerusalem, nor in the region of Judea in which the city of Jerusalem was located. Rather he traveled to Syria and Cilicia. Damascus was located in Syria, and Tarsus was located in Cilicia. Both cities represented birthplaces for Paul. His physical birth occurred in Tarsus of Cilicia, and his spiritual birth occurred in Damascus of Syria.

While spreading the gospel message to his places of origin, Paul developed a reputation among the churches of Judea. Read Galatians 1:22–24.

What was the report given about Paul?

____

____

____

What did these churches do as a result of this report?

____

____

____

Since Paul left Jerusalem and the region of Judea after only a short visit, he did not have time to share his message with the churches there. Rather he went to Cilicia and Syria, where the gospel message had not yet been widely preached. However, when the churches in Judea heard of Paul's conversion and his mission to spread the gospel, they formed an opinion of their own, not an opinion of Paul, but rather, an opinion of God.

As a result of Paul's conversion, they were able to see the Lord as a life-changing God, able to transform even the hardest of hearts. They were capable of viewing God as the true force behind this newfound faith to which they clung. They were able to see how human attempts to destroy God's new work were futile. And as a result, they praised God.

In Day One we discovered how God's opinion of Paul formed the basis of Paul's identity. In Day Two we were privy to both God's opinion and Paul's opinion of the Galatian church. Laden with grace, God's opinion gave the Galatians opportunity for hope. In Day Three, we observed the Galatians' weakness of following the opinions of others. In Day Four, we witnessed Paul's breakaway from the opinions of men, and in Day Five, we discover the true reward for pursuing only the opinions of God.

The true reward for pursuing God's opinion is a life that reflects God's glory. When we pursue God's opinion, we cause others to recognize God's work in our lives and his right to be praised. God is noticed, not us. When we are freed from the desire to please people and live life to please God, then we provide God the opportunity to receive the praise and glory. In reality, we step aside and no longer become the object of people's praise. Christ instead becomes the object of praise.

Read 2 Corinthians 3:18. What is happening to those who are reflecting the Lord's glory?

____

____

____

We are God's mirror image to the world. And a mirror that truly reflects God's glory is an indication that we are becoming more like him. When we follow other people's opinions, we reflect their glory and become more like them. But when we follow God's opinions, we reflect his glory and become more like him.

Take an honest look at your life; whose glory are you reflecting?

____

____

____

____

____

Prayer–*Lord, I think sometimes I reflect your glory, and other times I reflect others' glory. Of course, I'd rather reflect your glory at all times, because honestly, in the depths of my soul, I truly do want to be transformed into your image. I want to look like you, act like you, and be like you. Help me remember this whenever I'm tempted to succumb to the desire to please others.*

BREAKAWAY FROM THE ORDINARY

Galatians Chapter 2

VOW: "I have been crucified with Christ and I no longer live, but Christ lives in me. The life I live in the body, I live by faith in the Son of God, who loved me and gave himself for me."	Galatians 2:20

Day 1: An Extraordinary Alliance

Read Galatians 2:1–3.

When we last left Paul in Galatians 1, we saw him defending the origin of his gospel by proving his message came not from people, but from God. In our studies this week, we find him still in defense of his gospel. Yet, now his argument is no longer founded in the origin of his message, but rather in the fact that the early church leaders ratified his message. Paul substantiates his defense by rendering the details of his visit to Jerusalem, where he testified before the apostles.

Fortunately for Paul, he did not have to face these church leaders alone.

In her 2002 debut album entitled *Let Go,* soloist Avril Lavigne gave audiences a forewarning in her song "Anything But Ordinary." And since then, she's proven to be just that. Try as they might, the music industry has been unsuccessful in their attempts to shape this brazen twenty-two-year-old into the traditional mold of pop princess. From refusing to wear the revealing attire of her counterparts, to insisting she write her own music, Lavigne has snubbed the ordinary in pursuit of her own style, and in so doing, she's garnered a following.

Comparisons can be drawn between what Paul was to the Jews and what Avril Lavigne has been to the music industry. Paul was outspoken and straightforward and had a call to bring to the Gentiles a gospel that was anything but ordinary. And try as they might, the Jews could not force Paul into any kind of traditional mold. Nor could they influence him to instruct converted Gentiles to follow the law.

What did Paul do as recorded in Galatians 2:1, 2?

____

____

Galatians 2:16 presents a summary of the gospel Paul preached. Read this verse and describe the gospel Paul preached among the Gentiles.

____

____

____

This is no ordinary message. For centuries after the Jews had left Egypt, they followed the law Moses had received from God (Exodus 20–24). The law had been given at the inception of their nation and since then had become a prominent part of the Jews' religious heritage.

To further support his extraordinary gospel message, Paul opted to bring some of his friends with him to Jerusalem, where he met with the early church leaders. According to Galatians 2:1–3, who were his friends, and what was so unique about one friend in particular?

____

____

At the forefront of the debate over adherence to the law was the issue of circumcision. Circumcision is the cutting away of the male foreskin, and it was a requirement for any male converting to the Jewish faith. It was more than just an aspect of the law; it was evidence of a person's willingness to follow the *whole* law. Therefore, by requiring circumcision among New Testament believers, the Jews were binding those believers to adherence to the law.

Why do you think Paul brought Titus with him when he introduced his gospel to the leaders in Jerusalem?

____

____

____

When Avril Lavigne first caught the public eye, she wasn't clad in the scanty apparel of most young female singers in the music business. Instead she donned baggy pants, a wife-beater t-shirt, and a tie. Perhaps the most surprising thing about Lavigne's unusual appearance was it incited a trend that sent teen girls scrambling into the deep recesses of their fathers' closets to fish out their daily wardrobes.

As we study Galatians, we'll see that Paul's extraordinary calling and God-inspired message had incited a trend as well; a trend that sent pagan Gentiles into the unfamiliar territory of the Jewish faith in order to seek salvation from the Jews' God; a trend that had spawned Gentile believers throughout the Roman Empire.

Since a Gentile is anyone who isn't a Jew, Titus definitely fell within the Gentile category. And his presence in Jerusalem was representative of the countless converts who had come to Christ as a result of Paul's gospel.

Read Titus 1:4. How does Paul address Titus in this passage?

The message of the gospel that Paul preached surpassed cultural barriers and created a common bond among believers–a bond so tight, it superseded any other previous alliances.

Return to Galatians 1:18, 19 and identify the apostles Paul had previously met.

The men Paul saw in Galatians 1:18, 19 were some of the same men he met with privately in Galatians 2:2. These men were just like Paul. They were Jews. They were men whose call in life was to advance the message of Jesus Christ. By all right, Paul should have felt an immediate alliance with them. However, in this private meeting, Paul indicates an uncertainty regarding his fellow countrymen.

What was Paul afraid of according to Galatians 2:2?

Paul's primary fear was that if the leaders of the early church did not accept his message to the Gentiles, then a controversy could arise that would overshadow the importance of his ministry. For this reason, Paul opted to meet with the church leaders in private, before he made his appeal to a larger audience at the Jerusalem Council. Understand that Paul did not believe his message to the Gentiles was wrong or ill-conceived, nor was he planning to alter it if the leaders did not approve. He knew he was carrying out God's will. He just didn't want to present his calling to the council, only to have an argument arise among them and thereby threaten his ministry to the Gentiles. If such a division had occurred, then he could have been running his race in vain.

I do not wish to emphasize the picture of Paul running his race in vain, because thankfully, he did not. Instead I want to emphasize the fact that he did not have to run his race alone. According to Galatians 2:3, who was with him?

____

____

____

What an extraordinary alliance. Who would have thought a devout Jew like Paul and a pagan Gentile like Titus would have ever joined forces to confront the early church leaders with the novel concept that God wanted to save sinners of all races and tongues, independent of the law? But they did, and we'll discover the outcome of their alliance in Day Three.

With a skater persona and a bit of a tomboyish style, it would appear Avril Lavigne would have nothing in common with America's sweetheart, Kelly Clarkson. Since Clarkson is the product of America's largest talent search, *American Idol*, it would hardly seem likely that the Canadian-born songwriter, Lavigne, would have anything to do with her. And yet, somehow, they formed an extraordinary alliance with Clarkson's number one hit, "Breakaway." The song was co-written by Avril Lavigne and two others for Lavigne's album *Under My Skin.* However, Lavigne eventually decided not to release the song because she did not think it was a good fit for the album. Clarkson then gained possession of the song and later told New York radio station, Z100, that the song fit her life perfectly.

Apart, these two musicians appeal to two different audiences. Clarkson garners an older, more mature audience, while Lavigne appeals to a more rebellious, adolescent fan base. But together, they were able to make "Breakaway" an immediate success, perhaps because the song fit both of their lives–perfectly.

The gospel of salvation through Christ and not through the works of the law fit Paul's life perfectly. Having lived a life of bondage for so long under the law, Paul welcomed the freedom his newfound gospel provided. And Titus, whose life had been spent in bondage to a pagan society, must have found that the gospel message fit his life perfectly as well, because he was willing to forsake everything and form an alliance with Paul to advance the gospel message.

How has God's extraordinary gospel message reached beyond cultural barriers in your life and enabled you to form a common bond with people you would not normally associate with?

____

____

____

____

____

Prayer–*Lord, one thing is certain in my life. You are always stretching me, stretching me beyond my comfort zone to befriend others who either intimidate me or annoy me. But such uncommon friendships have allowed me glimpses of you and enabled me to see your ability to work in every life, even those lives that are the least like mine. Thank you for teaching me your grace and love through these friendships.*

Day 2: Defending the Extraordinary

Read Galatians 2:4–5.

Sometimes there's just no getting around a good fight. Or at least that's what Avril Lavigne indicated in her interview with *Newsweek* magazine when she recounted the details of a brawl she had with a guy she encountered at a record store. When his obscene comments about her failed to incite a tussle, he followed her outside the store. At this point, Lavigne took matters into her own hands and pummeled the guy right there on the sidewalk.[1]

Lavigne believed her honor was worth fighting for. Similarly, the apostle Paul, who was a little less "hands on" in his combative techniques, was just as resolute in his position that the gospel he preached to the Gentiles was worth fighting for. Today we will discover whom he fought with during his trip to Jerusalem when he addressed the Jerusalem Council. But first, it is important to read Luke's account of Paul's journey in the book of Acts. Luke's description offers us some insight as to why Paul traveled to Jerusalem in the first place and whom he clashed with while he was there.

1. Lorraine Ali, "Nobody's Fool," *Newsweek*, March 22, 2005, http://www.msnbc.msn.com/id/4522688.

☐ **Read Acts 15:1, 2. What events occurred that caused Paul to journey to Jerusalem?**

____

____

☐ **Read Acts 15:4, 5. In Jerusalem, Paul was met with opposition while at the Jerusalem Council. Who opposed him, and what did they insist needed to be done with the Gentile believers?**

____

____

☐ **How did Paul refer to his opponents in Galatians 2:4? And what was their intent?**

____

____

☐ **According to Galatians 2:5, how did Paul respond to these men?**

____

____

We will always have people who oppose our message or us in general. But Paul teaches us a lot in this passage. He shows us how to stand firm against the criticism and opposition we face. And most importantly, he gives us a great example of how to defend the extraordinary movement of God in our lives.

Like Paul, each of us possesses a unique quality, an unusual call, or an extraordinary gift. Avril Lavigne wrote about the extraordinary in her song "Anything But Ordinary," which is an ardent plea to be just that–anything but ordinary.

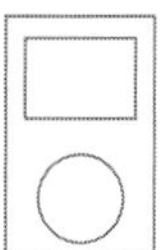

Interact with Your iPod®

Download Avril Lavigne's song, "Anything But Ordinary."

- Do you think you were created to be just ordinary? Or does God have a special calling for your life?
- Do you think Paul saw his mission in life as ordinary?

For Paul, the extraordinary was God's revealed truth; it was the gospel of salvation through grace apart from works. For us, the extraordinary is also God's revealed truth. Perhaps it's a job he's given us to do. Perhaps it's a dream or a career he's given us the desire for. Maybe it's a personal promise he's given us that we must defend against the voices of doubt and skepticism. Whatever it is, it's unique only to us, and therefore, to the rest of the world, it's extraordinary or even peculiar. Paul defended the extraordinary in his life. He defended it against the criticism of others. He upheld it despite opposition.

He didn't go on the attack while at the Jerusalem Council, but he stood firm and wouldn't let others dictate his decision. I think some of Paul's resolute behavior could be attributed to his personality. Because, let's face it, the man was hardheaded. (A trait I've often been accused of myself.)

Think of our first introduction to Paul (named Saul in this passage) in Acts 7:57, 58 and Acts 8:1. What is he doing here?

____

____

Paul's approval of Stephen's demise was pretty hardcore. Paul didn't flinch at a man's death. He didn't waiver in his resolve. He was thoroughly convinced he was right in his belief that the Jewish faith must be purged of dissident Christians. Later in Acts, we witness Paul's passion as he aggressively pursued the punishment of other Christians.

What is he doing in Acts 9:1, 2?

Sometimes I wonder if God loves to use a hardhead. Someone who goes full force after something regardless of whether it's right or wrong. A passionate person propelled onward by a dream, a vision, or a cause. I know God loves everyone, but I wonder if he has a soft spot in his heart for the more stubborn ones of this world. I mean, just think about what he told the church at Laodicea in Revelation 3:15, 16.

Write God's comments to the members of this church below.

In essence, he told them to make up their minds. If you're going to be hot, be hot with all your might. And if you're going to be cold, then go full force after it. But whatever you do, don't wallow in apathy and indifference. For goodness sakes, be passionately stubborn about something!

What are you passionate about?

____

____

____

____

____

____

Whatever you're passionate about could very well be your extraordinary call in life. Of course, there is always a downside to being passionately stubborn. As evidenced in Paul's early life as a Pharisee, there is the ever-present possibility that our passionate resolve is misguided. Despite his valiant efforts to eradicate Christians, Paul was dead wrong in his attempts. However, once God got a hold of him, Paul was right to be hardheaded about salvation by grace. So all in all, that's a fifty-percent success rate for an obstinate man who changed the course of human history.

According to Acts 9:3–9, what did Christ do to redirect Paul's passions?

____

____

____

The ultimate safety net for any Christian is a desire to please the Lord. That desire protects us and allows the Lord to give us a Damascus road encounter, just like Paul experienced. Christ was big enough to alter Paul's resolve. He was big enough to take a stubborn, hardheaded, passionate Pharisee like Paul and redirect him to a greater cause for which to be stubborn. Christ is capable of doing the same thing in our lives as long as the purpose of our passions is to please the Lord.

Prayer–*Lord, I think my greatest passion in life is to see people grow in you and in their knowledge of the Word. And that's why I constantly have to stand firm against the fear and insecurity that threaten to rob me of the extraordinary call you have on my life. I am scared and confused, and half the time I feel like giving up. Life would be so much easier if I just succumbed to the ordinary. Part of me longs to do just that. But the other part of me knows I was created for more. We all were. So please Lord, give us the courage to passionately and stubbornly pursue the extraordinary calls you have on each of our lives. And provide us with the faith to defend those calls when we're met with opposition.*

Day 3: Recognizing the Extraordinary

Read Galatians 2:6–10

Paul's main purpose for writing this epistle was to defend his extraordinary gospel message to the churches in Galatia. In Galatians 1, he proved his gospel was derived not from people, but from God. As we continue in our study of Galatians 2, we will see Paul's calling validated during the Jerusalem Council by the early church leaders: Peter, James (Jesus' half-brother), and John. And as Paul makes his case to the Galatians in our passage today, we're able to see how the early apostles recognized something extraordinary about Paul.

Paul makes reference to these early church leaders in Galatians 2:6. What does he have to say about people in high-profile positions?

____

____

Never one to be star-struck, Paul saw little need for pomp and circumstance when in the presence of the apostles. Avril Lavigne perhaps felt much the same way during a post-Grammy party attended by Hollywood's A-List. According to MTV correspondent SuChin Pak, Lavigne made little effort to impress the elite group of artists, executives, actors, and models in attendance. Adorned in a stained, sweaty shirt, her only accessory a skateboard that carried her across the asphalt parking lot, she appeared to be more intent on perfecting her ollie than she did on promoting her image.[2]

> The apostle James, whom Paul refers to in Galatians, should not be confused with John's brother, James, who was one of Christ's twelve disciples. At the time Galatians was written, John's brother, James, had already been martyred (Acts 12:1, 2). Therefore, when Paul refers to James in Galatians, he is referring to Christ's half-brother, who was the leader of the church in Jerusalem.

Paul knew he had been entrusted with an extraordinary call, and he did not allow his call to be confused with his image. Based on his comments about important people in Galatians 2:6, it's obvious Paul made little or no effort to impress the apostles at the Jerusalem Council. Their impression of him was not his main concern–the gospel he preached was.

According to Galatians 2:6, what did the apostles add to Paul's gospel message?

____

____

____

2. SuChin Pak, "Avril Lavigne: The Real Deal," *MTV News*, July 12, 2002, http://www.mtv.com/bands/l/lavigne_avril/news_feature_071202/index.jhtml.

In Galatians 2:7, 8, Paul comments that the apostles saw something peculiar about him. What was it the apostles saw?

According to Galatians 2:9, the apostles recognized something special had been given to Paul. What was it?

For a guy who wasn't concerned about his image, Paul sure received a lot of attention from the apostles. First they saw that he had been entrusted with the duty of bringing the gospel message to the Gentiles. I wonder how they recognized that calling upon Paul's life. Paul's writings don't indicate any intent to impress the apostles. On the contrary, Paul wrote in Galatians 2:2 how he merely arrived in Jerusalem and "set before them the gospel that I preach among the Gentiles." He did not first attempt to sell himself or his credibility. He merely "set before them the gospel."

The second thing the apostles recognized about Paul was that grace had been given to him. Grace is basically God giving us something we do not deserve. To understand the extent of this grace, it is important to study the fruit of Paul's ministry.

Return to Acts 15, which also records the events of Paul's journey to Jerusalem. In verse 12, what did Paul (and Barnabas) tell the assembly during the Jerusalem Council?

After hearing the miracles God had done through Paul and Barnabas, the assembly of apostles in Jerusalem first recognized Paul's extraordinary call to bring the gospel to the Gentiles. And next, they recognized the grace given to Paul in order to fulfill that call.

We give people the opportunity to recognize God's grace and his extraordinary call on our lives when we take the leap of faith to operate in that call. Had Paul not first trusted God to work through him in his ministry to the Gentiles, then he would have had nothing to offer the apostles at the Jerusalem Council.

What are some steps you can take to ensure others recognize God's call on your life?

____

____

____

____

____

____

____

____

Think about the people in your small group. Can you recognize God's call on each of their lives? If so, state your observations below.

____

____

____

As a result of the things they recognized, the apostles gave Paul (and Barnabas) something. Galatians 2:9 mentions this gift. What was it, and what did they commission Paul to go and do?

This act of affirmation by the early church leaders would have held a great deal of influence with the Galatian churches to whom Paul was writing. In his defense of his calling, Paul was able to remind the churches of Galatia that, indeed, the early church leaders, James, Peter, and John, had not only affirmed his calling, but had commissioned him to spread the good news of Jesus Christ throughout the Gentile world.

When people recognize the calling God has for our lives, it allows an opportunity for the spread of the gospel. Maybe not in the direct form Paul's gospel was spread, but perhaps in more subtle ways. Perhaps through our passionate pursuit of God's purpose for our lives, others are able to recognize that true purpose in life is found through Christ. Or possibly through our determination to fight the fear that holds us back from operating in our calls, others recognize that "God has not given us a spirit of fear, but of power and of love and of a sound mind" (2 Timothy 1:7, NKJV).

I know a sweet couple whose baby was born with abnormalities. I watch them carry her from doctor to doctor because she has so many needs that require specialists. And through it all, they maintain a strong faith in the Father. That couple has an extraordinary call on their lives, a call to love and care for a child who may never be capable of reciprocating their love. Yet they have the courage to operate in their call, and, in so doing, the message of Christ's unconditional love for us is demonstrated.

Prayer–*Oh God, thank you for people who are unafraid to walk in your extraordinary call for their lives. Thank you for the way you make yourself recognizable through them. I want to be that kind of person. I want others to be able to recognize you and your call on my life. So please, give me the courage to pursue your extraordinary call for me.*

Day 4: The Allure of the Ordinary

Read Galatians 2:11–14

What conflict occurs in Galatians 2:11?

____

____

In his attempts to persuade the Galatian churches of the truth of his gospel, Paul was not content to merely state that his gospel had originated from God (Galatians 1). Nor was it enough for him to recount the events of the Jerusalem Council where James, Peter, and John affirmed his gospel. Paul thought it necessary to provide the Galatians with further evidence by relaying to them how he used his gospel to correct the apostle Peter.

Read John 21:15–17.

What was Peter asked repeatedly in these verses?

____

____

What was his response?

What was he commissioned to do?

According to Galatians 2:7, what had Peter been entrusted with?

Peter had a dual calling in life. Not only was he entrusted with the responsibility of preaching the gospel to unbelieving Jews, he was also commissioned to disciple those who were already followers of Christ. But during his stay in the Gentile city of Antioch, he made a grave mistake, one that endangered both his witness and his ability to feed Christ's sheep.

What was Peter's mistake according to Galatians 2:12, 13?

Remember Avril Lavigne's song "Anything But Ordinary"? (If you don't, then listen to it again.) What did you like about it?

What did it make you want to do?

I like Lavigne's song because she makes the idea of being unique and extraordinary sound so enticing, so rebellious, and so alive. But when the novelty of being "anything but ordinary" wears off and the attention we get from being different turns into criticism, it's easy to succumb to the ordinary. At that point, the ordinary is alluring.

According to verse 12, when men representing James arrived in Antioch, Peter changed his behavior toward Gentiles. Why did he do this?

While in Antioch, Peter was allured by the ordinary. And the primary cause for his departure from the extraordinary was fear. Fear will always attempt to keep us from pursuing God's extraordinary call on our lives. In this passage, Peter was faced with a fear of others. He was fearful of what others might say about him, so he temporarily abandoned the responsibilities of his extraordinary call.

I've encountered much the same fears. I fear what others think about me all the time. But perhaps the most stifling fear in my life right now is a fear of failure. It is an unwanted companion on my journey toward the extraordinary–ever tempting me to give up, preserve my dignity, and fade into the throng of people who have contented themselves with the ordinary.

What fears attempt to dissuade you from pursuing the extraordinary?

____

____

____

____

____

____

Fear is the antithesis of faith. We can't step out in faith if we've chosen to remain stagnant in fear. Fortunately for Peter, Paul called him on his fear (see verse 14). The whole incident surely bruised Peter's ego, but it protected his extraordinary call.

Recall Peter's conversation with Christ in John 21. Why do you think Christ asked Peter if he loved him?

____

____

____

Theologians agree that the reason Christ asked Peter three times if he loved him was in order to reinstate Peter after his denial of Christ (see John 18). But I believe there was more to it than that. Of course Christ wanted Peter to verbally affirm his love for him, but I also think Christ wanted Peter personally to realize that his love for Christ had not wavered in spite of his earlier denials. Though Peter's denials had been motivated by fear, Christ knew the apostle's heart possessed a deep, abiding love for the Lord. Therefore, in his final exchange with Peter, Christ redirected Peter's focus from his fears to his first love.

Write 1 John 4:18 below.

In her song, "Anything But Ordinary," Avril Lavigne asks her audience if it truly is enough to love. When fear makes the ordinary alluring and we are in danger of forsaking God's extraordinary call on our lives, a love for God is our lifeline. In fact, Christ told the Pharisees in Matthew 22:37, 38 that the first and greatest commandment is to love the Lord God with all our heart, soul, and mind. A perfect, ever-trusting love for God doesn't just protect us from fear; it casts it out.

Fear causes us to focus on ourselves, but love redirects our attention to the object of our affection. When we truly love the Lord, our love for him becomes more important than our fear. There is no way we can manifest a pure, perfect love for God on our own. But thankfully Romans 5:5 promises that, "God has poured out his love into our hearts by the Holy Spirit." Therefore, all we need do is accept this love and allow our focus to reside upon the One we love. When God enables us to do this, then our fears fall by the wayside and we're able to answer Avril Lavigne's question in the affirmative. Yes . . . it is enough to love.

Prayer–*Lord, I am so much like Peter, often forgetting whom I love and falling prey to fear. I want to daily ask myself the question you addressed to Peter in John 21:15: "Peter, do you love me more than these?" God, Peter was surrounded by his closest friends when you asked him that question, and yet he still responded with, "Yes, Lord." Give me the courage to do the same whenever I am paralyzed by a fear of man. And when a fear of failure bombards my thoughts, allow my love for you to protect me. Give me a perfect love for you, a love that casts out my fears and allows me to run after you.*

Day 5: "The Cost of the Extraordinary"

Read Galatians 2:15–21.

Some of the verses we will study today are quotes from Paul's lecture to Peter in Antioch. I'm not sure if Paul included his reprimand of Peter in Galatians because he wanted the churches of Galatia to know exactly what he'd spoken to the famous apostle, or because his argument was so well-executed it was too irresistible to omit. But one thing is certain; Paul introduces the main theme of Galatians in this rebuke.

Read Galatians 2:15–17 and fill in the blanks below for verse 16.

". . . know that a man is not justified by observing the law, but by faith in Jesus Christ. So we, too, have put our ____________ in Christ Jesus that we may be ______________ by ____________ in Christ and not by observing the law, because by observing the law no one will be justified."

–Galatians 2:16

Study the above verse. What words are repeated?

What theme is repeated twice?

Paul had a thing for repetition. Maybe he knew his audience would learn by repetition, so he repeated key words numerous times throughout the text of Galatians. These repetitive words in verse 16 summarize the main theme of Galatians: *We are justified by faith in Christ and not by observing the law.*

> The Greek word often translated "justification" is *dikaioo,* and this word is used eight times in Galatians. One of the Greek words translated "faith" in the New Testament is *pistis,* which is used twenty times throughout this book. The Greek word *nomos* is translated "law" in the New Testament, and it is used a total of twenty-five times in Galatians.

In his commentary on Galatians, Warren Wiersbe writes, "Justification is the act of God whereby he declares the believing sinner righteous in Jesus Christ."[3] As Paul recounts to the Galatians his rebuke of Peter, Paul argues we are not declared righteous by our observance of the law, but rather by our faith in Christ. What an extraordinary situation! Even though we are sinners, God declares us righteous, merely by our faith in Jesus Christ.

Read Galatians 2:18–21. Pay close attention to the personal pronouns Paul uses in these verses. What is different about the pronouns in

3. Warren Wiersbe, *Be Free* (Colorado Springs: Cook Communications, 2005), 53.

these verses compared to the personal pronouns Paul uses in verses 15–17? (In case you're not an English major, personal pronouns are: ***I, you, he, she, it, we, me, they, him, her, us, and them.*****)**

In verses 15–17 Paul is executing a skillful defense meant to convince his audience of justification by faith. But in verses 18–21 things become more personal. These verses may refer to Paul's reprimand of Peter, but they weren't just points in an analytical debate. They were a part of Paul. They were more than just his passion; they were his very reason to live.

What does Paul have to say about his mortality in verse 19?

In her song "Anything But Ordinary," Avril Lavigne also mentions mortality. After a somewhat graphic description of heart extraction, she wonders if death is enough. For Paul, it wasn't just enough for him to die to the law and the slavery of trying to follow it. Prior to knowing Christ, the law had been his life, his reason for living. His passion for the law once fueled his hatred of Christians and dictated his hostilities against them. As passionate as Paul was, death to the law would have never been enough. He had to have a reason to live.

What was Paul's reason to live according to verse 19?

When Paul ceased his vain attempts to justify himself through the law, he was then truly able to live for something greater than the law; he was capable of living for the Lawgiver. He no longer needed the law to mediate his relationship with God because Christ became his mediator, thus allowing Paul the opportunity for a personal, intimate relationship with the living God.

Paul expounds on his death and life in verse 20. How does Paul describe his symbolic death?

Read Luke 23:39–41. Consider the two men crucified with Christ.

What qualified them for crucifixion? Did they get what they deserved?

In her song, all Avril Lavigne wants is to be anything but ordinary. Sin makes us so ordinary. Romans 3:23 tells us, "all have sinned." Therefore, in order to become truly extraordinary, we must first admit we are sinners, deserving physical death and in need of forgiveness. Next, we must be willing to accept Christ's death on the cross as the payment for our sins. These two steps assure us of our salvation and an eternity with God.

But Paul took his relationship with the Almighty to a new level. Salvation was not enough for him. He needed more. He needed to experience death–not just death to the law, but death to self.

In Galatians 2:20, who does Paul say lives within him?

The cost of being extraordinary is death. The most extraordinary individual in the world is someone who has died to his or her own selfish desires and lives instead for the desires of another. We as Christians are given the opportunity to die to ourselves and live for the desires of Christ. And because Christ dwells in us, we have the assurance that he's not scrutinizing us from heaven and awaiting our mistakes. He's within us, guiding us.

Have you accepted Christ as your Savior, allowing him the opportunity to live within you, guiding you through your life's course? If so, you are anything but ordinary.

It requires faith to believe Christ lives within us, guiding us. Perhaps that is why Paul wrote in verse 20, "The life I live in the body, I live by faith in the Son of God." One of the most extraordinary people in history, Martin Luther, expounded on Paul's writings in his commentary on Galatians:

> "I live by the faith of the Son of God," he (Paul) says. "My speech is no longer directed by the flesh, but by the Holy Ghost. My sight is no longer governed by the flesh, but by the Holy Ghost. My hearing is no longer determined by the flesh, but by the

Holy Ghost. I cannot teach, write, pray, or give thanks without the instrumentality of the flesh; yet these activities do not proceed from the flesh, but from God."[4]

I like Martin Luther's view of living by faith while still living in the flesh. What does living by faith look like in your life?

Prayer–*Father, I'm learning that living an extraordinary life is more than just taking chances or even trying to fulfill your call for me. Living an extraordinary life means allowing you to live my life for me. It means living by faith and allowing you the opportunity to guide me and control me. Help me surrender all I am to you. Help my life's motto to be Christ's attitude in the Garden of Gethsemane, "Yet not what I will, but what you will" (Mark 14:36).*

4. Martin Luther, *A Commentary on St. Paul's Epistle to the Galatians* (Grand Rapids, MI: Christian Classics Ethereal Library, 1949), 47. http://www.ccel.org/ccel/luther/galatians.pdf.

Galatians Chapter 3

VOW: "Clearly no one is justified before God by the law, because, 'The righteous will live by faith.'"	Galatians 3:11

Day 1: "Bewitched by Doubt"

Read Galatians 3:1–5.

Galatians 3 is an exciting chapter because it marks a turning point in Paul's letter. No longer does Paul defend his ministry as he did in the first two chapters. This week we focus on Paul addressing the heart of the Galatians' problem, the very issue that caused them to turn from the truth of the gospel in the first place.

No one would suspect one of the top bands in the UK to be riddled with doubt. But the group Coldplay, or at least their lead singer, Chris Martin, is. After the release of their second album, *A Rush of Blood to the Head,* in August 2002, *MTV News* quoted Martin as saying,

> not a single night goes past where I don't wake up sweating and thinking no one will like this record. We poured every ounce of soul, emotion and love into it, and now we can only wait and see.[1]

Despite Martin's phobia, *A Rush of Blood to the Head* received high acclaims from critics at *Entertainment Weekly*, *Rolling Stone*, and *Billboard.* In addition, it won Best British Album at the British Awards in London and it received the Q Award for Best Album in October of 2002, beating out the work of Red Hot Chili Peppers for the title. In 2003, the winning continued with three Grammy Awards and a host of honors at the NME Bash.

Martin doubted the truth. The truth was that Coldplay's previous album, *Parachutes,* released in 2000, had been well-received by fans, and its successor, *A Rush of Blood to the Head,* was embraced with equal enthusiasm. Martin's neurosis is not uncommon among musicians, but for him, it was a crippling weight to bear. The Galatians also suffered beneath the burden of doubt. Just like Chris Martin, they doubted the truth.

Read Galatians 3:1–5.

Observe the phrases Paul repeatedly compares in verses 2 and 5. What are these phrases?

____

____

____

____

____

1. Jon Wiederhorn, "Coldplay Bleed for Beauty on *A Rush of Blood to the Head,*" interview with Chris Martin, *MTV News,* August 27, 2002, http://www.vh1.com/artists/news/1457204/08272002/coldplay.jhtml.

Since we're only privy to Paul's side of the argument, we have to study his responses to the Galatians in order to determine their dilemma. Why do you think Paul asked them these questions?

In Week Two, we noted that Avril Lavigne's song "Anything But Ordinary" repeatedly asks "if it was enough"–if loving, breathing, and dying were enough. The Galatians were also caught in a quest for sufficiency and likewise doubted if it was enough–if belief in Christ was really enough. In response to their uncertainty, Paul specifically asks them questions that cause them to compare the truth of the gospel with the lie they had chosen to believe.

Read Galatians 3:1 again.

How does Paul refer to the Galatians in verse 1?

What question does he ask them?

The Galatians lived in metropolitan cities influenced by Greek philosophy that esteemed wisdom and knowledge above all else. The label of "fool" would have certainly bruised the egos of these early Christians immersed in such an intellectual society. Paul's choice of words was especially painful since *anoetos,* the Greek word translated "foolish" in this chapter, really means "lacking in the power of perception, unwise."[2]

The Galatians' lack of perception made them vulnerable to the deceit of the Judaizers. If you remember from Week One, we learned the Judaizers were a group of people who claimed to be Christians but required adherence to the law as a true indicator of salvation and righteousness. Their presence in the Galatian church "bewitched" Paul's converts.

While the Galatian cities within the Roman Empire were influenced by the intellectualism of Greek culture, they were also steeped in superstition. Therefore, Paul uses a mystic term when addressing the Galatians. The Greek word translated "bewitched" in verse 1 is indicative of the "evil eye." People in the first century believed a spell could be cast by staring into a person's evil eye. It refers to the method by which a serpent charms or hypnotizes its prey.

Turn to Genesis 3:1. Think about how the serpent charmed Eve. Did he lie to her, or did he merely cause her to question the truth?

___

___

___

Satan bewitched Eve by casting doubt on the truth of God's words. Eve's doubt led to her sin. When seeking to deceive the Galatians, the enemy utilized the same tactic and bewitched them with doubt. Paul's questions in the first five verses of chapter 3 convey the depth of the Galatians' doubt as to whether faith in Christ was enough.

2. Kenneth Wuest, *Wuest's Word Studies from the Greek New Testament: Volume One* (Grand Rapids: Wm. B. Eerdmans Publishing Company, 1973), 83.

Think of a time in your life when you have been plagued with doubt. Describe the situation that caused you to doubt the truth.

____

____

____

____

____

____

There was a time in my life when doubting the truth led to my being deceived. It began quite innocently in high school. Most girls that age are consumed with their weight, and I was no different–a diet here, a workout there, a missed meal every now and again. All seemed perfectly natural–until I began avoiding meals more frequently and started binging and purging.

At first I assumed my behavior was normal, but in college things continued, only with more intensity. The binges were so great my "Freshman Fifteen" (extra pounds) was more like a Freshman Fifty. My job as a waitress made food more available and gave me greater opportunity to binge, which only increased my guilt. And like clockwork, the guilt always prompted the purging.

I had grown up memorizing scripture. A passage that I don't even remember learning, but have always seemed to know, was the greatest commandment found in Matthew 22:37–39:

> "Love the Lord your God with all your heart and with all your soul and with all your mind." This is the first and greatest commandment. And the second is like it: "Love your neighbor as yourself."

When I was younger, I doubted that scripture. Not the commandments to love God or love my neighbor; those both seemed like rather noble principles. But the commandment to love myself was a little doubtful. In fact, to me, it seemed like true virtue was found in actually disliking myself rather than risking the peril of pride by actually liking myself, or heaven forbid, loving myself.

So eventually, my doubt led me to turn from the truth. Believing the only way to truly attain righteousness was to dislike and even despise myself, I allowed that lie to fuel my sin of self-hatred, which subsequently led to my bulimia.

Doubt is like a welcome mat at the doorstep of deceit. It greets us and ushers us onward toward the enemy's lies. At the time Galatians was written, the church in Galatia had moved beyond the welcome mat and passed through the portal to embrace deception.

Write the truths found in the following scriptures.

Psalm 139:14

____

____

Isaiah 41:10

____

____

Jeremiah 29:11

____

____

Romans 10:9

Ephesians 1:4

Which of these truths are you most likely to doubt? Why?

Thankfully, the Lord knows our tendency toward doubt. I think that's why he allowed someone by the name of John Mark to include in his gospel the story of Christ's healing of a young boy. The story found in Mark 9:14–29 can teach us a great deal about faith and doubt.

Review this story and write the father's response to Jesus in verse 24.

Prayer—*Lord, I'm often tempted to doubt Ephesians 1:4. Believing that you chose me to be in Christ before the foundation of the world is mind-boggling, but it's a little easier to accept than the second part of that truth. The part that incites my skepticism is the part about being holy and blameless in your sight. That's so hard for me to believe, especially since I most definitely don't feel holy and blameless. I feel rather sinful at times to be honest. Sometimes I wish I had the faith to see myself through your eyes and to embrace the truth you speak about me. Please give me that faith Lord. I believe, but help my unbelief.*

Day 2: Dispelling Doubt

Read Galatians 3:6–14.

In our focus passage of Galatians, the apostle Paul directs his readers to "consider Abraham." Scholars believe Paul used the patriarch Abraham as an example of faith because the Judaizers had convinced the Galatians that salvation was through direct association with Abraham's descendants. Since Abraham was the father of the Jewish nation, Jews often mistakenly believed their salvation was guaranteed because of their relationship to Abraham. The Judaizers had encouraged the Gentiles in Galatia to observe the law in order to be consistent with the Jewish faith and thus become heirs of Abraham.

In our focus passage, Paul refutes this doctrine. What is the first thing Paul says about Abraham in Galatians 3:6?

____

____

____

Read Galatians 3:7. What does Paul say the qualifications are for being a child of Abraham?

___

___

The first thing Paul does to dispel the Galatians' doubt is to point them toward the truth of the Word. Paul explains to the Galatians in verses 8 and 9 that God promised Abraham that all the nations would be blessed through him. That promise is beneficial not only to Jews, but to Gentiles as well. Therefore, it is not necessary for Gentiles to convert to Judaism, because salvation is not dependent upon national heritage or religious rites; it is dependent upon faith.

In verses 10 through 14, Paul offers yet another argument for salvation by faith instead of by the works of the law. He mentions how the law brings a curse, but Christ came to redeem us from that curse so that we might live by faith. But what does it really mean to live by faith?

After their successful debut album, *Parachutes,* Coldplay found it increasingly difficult to live by faith. So doubtful were they of their ability to recapture their previous accomplishments, the band considered breaking up. But they realized they had one more contribution to the music world when they came up with the song, "In My Place." Chris Martin commented on "In My Place," stating, "that was the one thing on the horizon that we thought, 'We must stay together for that.' And we did, and that's why we're still here."[3]

Coldplay displayed faith in their song "In My Place," and that faith prompted them to produce another album. Faith can be a powerful force, pushing us beyond our boundaries and leading us to accomplish things we never dreamed possible. But faith is a treasure

3. Jon Wiederhorn, "Coldplay On, Thanks to New Single," interview with Coldplay, *MTV News,* August 13, 2002, http://www.vh1.com/artists/news/1456991/08122002/coldplay.jhtml.

that must be fiercely protected, especially during the waiting period. When a dream is first conceived or a promise first made, the hardest part is waiting for its fulfillment. It is during the wait that the doubt must be dispelled.

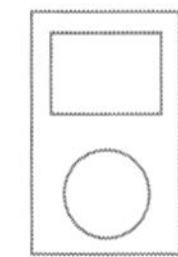

Interact with Your iPod®

Download Coldplay's song "In My Place."

- Does this song make you want to wait for something special?
- Does it describe your feelings while you're waiting for the fulfillment of a dream or promise?

I gotta be honest, this song is way too deep for me, and I really don't understand it. But fortunately, Coldplay explained the song to CNN reporter Joanne Suh as being about your position in the world.[4] The Judaizers wanted the Gentiles to believe their position in the world was outside the bounds of God's promises to Abraham, and perhaps, before the coming of Christ, it was.

But after years and years of waiting, the Gentiles were offered an opportunity to be a part of those promises through faith in Christ. Yet instead of depending on faith, the Galatians became dependent upon their own ability to follow the law. In his letter, Paul attempts to dispel the Galatians' doubts about faith by teaching them the truth of God's Word and by referring to Abraham's faith.

4. Joanne Suh, "Coldplay Uses Its 'Head,'" CNN's *Showbiz Today*, August 30, 2002, http://www.cnn.com/CNN/Programs/showbiz.today/music.ontheroad/0208/30.html.

Let's consider Abraham's faith and how he dealt with doubt during his waiting period in Genesis 15:9–11. What did Abraham (referred to as Abram in this passage) do with the birds of prey?

As recorded in this passage, God had just promised Abraham the land of Canaan. To confirm this oath, God cut a covenant with Abraham. In those days, covenants, or promises, were made by placing the halves of dead animals opposite each other with both parties walking between the halves. It signified that if either party broke the covenant, they would meet the same demise as the animals through which they walked.

> Normally, both parties walked between the animals. This symbolized their joint responsibility in the fulfillment of the covenant. But in Genesis 15, only the presence of God entered between the animal halves, evidence of God's ultimate responsibility in the fulfillment of the promise.

While Abraham waited for the presence of God to return to him, birds of prey came in to devour the symbols of God's promise. The Judaizers were to the Galatians like birds of prey, robbing them of the promises of God. Instead of driving them away like Abraham did, the Galatians entertained them, considered their arguments, and finally fell prey to them.

Identify the birds of prey that threaten to rob you of your faith in God's promises. What are they?

Just like Abraham, we too will have to endure a waiting period. And as we wait for God's promises to be fulfilled in our lives, remember that our position in the world should always be one of faith, standing guard against the birds of prey that cause us to doubt God and his plan for our lives.

Prayer—*Lord, sometimes the birds of prey in my life come in the form of unmet expectations. When I assume you're going to do something at a certain time and then you don't do it, I begin to doubt you. I know that's not fair to you, nor is it really based on a faith in you. Rather, it's based on my faith that you'll give me what I want when I want it. And that's not true faith. True faith is saying I believe you to do what you deem best for me in your timing. So Father, forgive me for allowing my unmet expectations to become birds of prey in my life, robbing me of my faith in you.*

Day 3: Don't Doubt the Promise

Read Galatians 3:15–20.

In 2004, after two hit albums, Coldplay returned to the studio to record a third album, *X & Y*. But their time in the recording studio proved to be more difficult than they had anticipated. Chris Martin told BBC News that Coldplay's first eight months in the studio were spent in vain, producing substandard songs.[5] Unwilling to succumb to mediocrity, Coldplay determined to offer fans the finest musical fare possible. So they extended their recording session, and subsequently delayed the release of their album by three months.

5. "Coldplay Attack 'Corporate Evil,'" *BBC News*, May 18, 2005, http://news.bbc.co.uk/1/hi/entertainment/music/4557877.stm.

When the band failed to meet their release deadline, Coldplay's British-owned production company, EMI, issued a warning to shareholders citing a decline in profits and attributed the decline to Coldplay's delays. Despite EMI's profit margin, Coldplay determined to produce a top-notch CD, even if that meant the album would be released in June 2005 instead of March.

In our focus passage for Day Three, Paul continues to defend his claim that salvation by faith was available to the Galatians. To support his claim, Paul uses the argument that a promise is a promise, no matter what.

Read Galatians 3:15. What does Paul say about a human covenant?

____

____

____

Paul's use of an enduring human covenant to substantiate his claim was much more effective in the first century when human covenants were not easily altered. Today contracts are written, rewritten, renegotiated, and amended with increasing regularity. Coldplay's dealings with their production company evidence this fact, because Coldplay opted to modify their covenant with little difficulty. Despite EMI's protests, Coldplay added an extra three months to their human covenant with the famed production company. Fortunately for Coldplay, they had enough clout in the music industry to keep the third largest production company in the world waiting.

When you think about it, God had enough clout to alter his promise to humanity. He could have decided he wanted salvation to be based on our efforts instead of on his. He could have made us work for our salvation, instead of just believing him for it, but he didn't. What he did do was keep us waiting–waiting for the Messiah to come and fulfill the promise–but then again, he never said he wouldn't make us wait. And while we were waiting, God gave mankind the Mosaic Law.

What does Paul have to say about the law in Galatians 3:17?

____

____

____

The promise Paul refers to in this passage is God's promise to bless all the nations of the world through Abraham. In other words, God promised Abraham that all people would be provided the opportunity to become God's children through Abraham's descendant, Jesus Christ. Salvation would be available to all people, regardless of national heritage, through their faith in Jesus Christ (see Genesis 12:1–3).

The Judaizers had taught the Galatians to believe that the introduction of the Mosaic Law changed the original promise God made with Abraham. But Paul refuted this by stating that the law did not invalidate the covenant God previously made.

Read Galatians 3:19.

What was the purpose of the law?

____

____

How long was the law supposed to last?

____

____

This is the first of two points Paul makes regarding the insufficiency of the law in comparison to the promise. The first point he makes is that the Mosaic Law was added for a specific purpose and for a specific period. The law's specified purpose was to make man aware of his sin. The law's specified period of dominance began on Mt. Sinai in Exodus, and this period ended on Golgotha when Christ, the promised seed, met all the requirements of the law by becoming the perfect sacrifice for mankind's sins. The benefits of the law were temporal, unlike the promise of the seed, which is eternal.

Read Galatians 3:19, 20. How was the law put into effect?

____

____

Secondly, Paul argues that a mediator was used for the giving of the law, while during the giving of the promise, God himself orchestrated the details. The very fact that God mediated the promise himself was evidence of the importance God placed upon his eternal covenant with Abraham.

Paul's two points about the law give us insight into the things that are really important to God. First, we can learn that while God is concerned with the temporary, he is much more interested in the eternal. Secondly, when God makes an important promise, he personally sets out to make good on it. We must cherish the things that are eternal along with the personal promises God makes to us. We must fiercely guard these against the doubt the enemy sends our way.

Our salvation is the most important possession in our lives. It is both eternal and mediated by God. Consider your salvation. Have you ever been tempted to doubt it?

____

____

As a Christian, why do you think doubting your salvation is so dangerous?

Think about the Galatian church. What caused them to turn away from the true gospel and follow the teachings of the Judaizers?

Doubting our salvation can cause us to look elsewhere for deliverance. The Galatians' doubt led them to pursue salvation through good works instead of through God's grace and acceptance. But constantly doubting our salvation can lead to other perils as well.

A few years ago I wrote a study on Hebrews. And as I was writing the study, the Lord allowed me to encounter some difficult truths about myself. (As is so often the case when God uses me to do something, he doesn't let me mess with other people's lives until he first messes with mine!) He revealed to me that I had spent the majority of my Christian experience worrying and fretting over my salvation, doubting whether I was saved or whether I wasn't, wondering if a certain act would nullify my salvation and send me to hell. I know it sounds crazy, but I spent an amazing amount of spiritual energy doubting my salvation.

Thankfully, God showed me Hebrews 5:11–6:1, which basically says, "Grow up and move on to more mature things." By doubting my salvation I was stunting my spiritual growth. (A pretty scary revelation for me since I was actually writing a Bible study at the time.)

I wasn't concerned with moving on in my relationship with the Lord because I was still questioning whether or not I had one. Well, I take that back; I did believe I had a relationship with God. I was just worried I might do something to mess it up, and that kind of mentality can be exhausting. And according to Hebrews, it's rather immature.

Now when it comes to my salvation, I rest in the words Paul wrote to Timothy in 2 Timothy 1:12, "Yet I am not ashamed, because I know whom I have believed, and am convinced that he is able to guard what I have entrusted to him for that day."

Thousands of years ago, God made a promise to Abraham to bless the nations through Abraham's descendant, Jesus Christ. When I asked Jesus into my heart, I became a part of that promise, and now I rest in the confidence that God is able to guard me and my commitment to him. I now refuse to allow doubt to rob me of that assurance. Besides, if God is able to keep a several-thousand-year-old promise to Abraham, he's certainly more than capable of keeping my salvation for the short time I'm on this earth.

Prayer–*Father, I have so much for which to be thankful. But today, I want to express to you my sincere gratitude for my salvation. Thank you for keeping your promise to Abraham so that I could be a part of that promise. Thank you that you are able to keep that which I have entrusted to you–my very heart and my salvation. Thank you that I am eternally yours.*

Day 4: The Faith to Step Out

Read Galatians 3:21–25.

Christopher Anthony John Martin grew up as the eldest of five in a working-class family. His father was an accountant, and his mother a schoolteacher. He was given a privileged education at the Sherwood School for boys, whose alumni list boasts a host of famous actors, politicians, and journalists. Upon graduation, Chris Martin made his way to London, where he attended University College of London, majoring in ancient history. But little did he know that during his first week of college, his dreams of becoming an ancient history teacher would be forever altered.

The Judaizers believed that with the introduction of the Mosaic Law, God's plan for humanity had been forever altered. They assumed that the law was contrary to the promise of God and therefore nullified the promise. They had taught these untruths to the Galatians, who were now in a quandary over the whole issue. Understanding their dilemma, Paul addressed the Galatians in verse 21.

What question does Paul ask in Galatians 3:21?

____

____

What answer does he give in response to his question?

____

____

What does Paul say the purpose of the law is in verse 24?

____

____

In the New American Standard Bible, verse 24 says, "the law has become our tutor to lead us to Christ." The word tutor in this passage is from the Greek word *paidagogos* meaning "a child conductor." This word is the ancestor of the English word "pedagogue." In Paul's day, a well-educated slave would be given charge of the child in the household. The slave's responsibility was to provide oversight of the child by protecting him, guiding him to and from school, disciplining him when needed, and also teaching him on occasion. The child was not born to the slave, nor did he belong to the slave–but the slave brought him up. The slave taught him right from wrong. Romans 3:20 tells us that "through the law we become conscious of sin." The whole purpose of the law was similar to that of the slave–to show us the difference between right and wrong.

> Paul uses the analogy of a pedagogue to reveal to the Galatians the law's role in Israel's upbringing. God chose Israel to be a special people because he intended for the Messiah to come from the Jewish nation. To teach the Jews right from wrong, he gave them the Mosaic Law; however, he never intended for them to belong to this law, but merely to be brought up by it.

Not only was the law given to reveal right from wrong, it was also given to convince us of our inability to fulfill the law, thus making us painfully aware of our need for a Savior. That's why Paul said the law was meant to lead us to Christ. It was meant to reveal to us our inadequacies so we would accept the hope offered through Jesus Christ.

During his first week of college, Chris Martin met Jon Buckland, Will Champion, and Guy Berryman. At first their common interest in rock music seemed but a mere distraction from their studies. Buckland, who started playing the guitar at age eleven, studied astronomy and mathematics. Champion, who studied anthropology, spent most of his time at UCL teaching himself how to play the drums since their hodge-podge band needed a percussionist. And Berryman, who aspired to be an engineer, dropped out after a year in order to hone his talents on the bass guitar and focus on playing with Coldplay.

All four band members entered London's University College for different reasons, yet somehow their acceptance into the university led them to a greater destination, a destination that required their departure from UCL. Had they all remained at University College, they may have earned their degrees, but they would have forfeited their destinies.

According to Galatians 3:25, what happens now that faith has come?

____

____

Paul's greatest concern was that the Galatians would hold so tightly to the law–the process that was meant to lead them to Christ–that they would forfeit their destiny with Christ. The law was meant to be a part of their upbringing, but it wasn't meant to guide them forever. At some point, they needed to step out in faith.

Much like the law, University College served a specific purpose in the lives of the band members of Coldplay. It was the catalyst that brought them together, but for them to remain there would have been detrimental to their success as a band.

Think about your life. Have you ever experienced something that was initially beneficial for you but would have eventually hindered your growth?

____

____

____

____

____

____

My spiritual growth has not necessarily been threatened by a location or a life stage, but rather by a relationship. As I write this study, I suffer from loss–the loss of a mentor. I wish I could say life without her has made me stronger, but all it has done is allow me to recognize my dependence. For a while, God permitted me to learn from her and be dependent upon her, but only for a season. Once that season was over, he allowed her to be removed from my life so I would not confuse dependence on her with dependence on him. I have no doubt she was a part of my spiritual growth process, but to remain with her much longer would have been detrimental to my development.

I miss her so much. I miss her encouragement and validation. I doubt every day whether I can write this Bible study without her influence in my life. God has moved her on and is using her in a mighty way in others' lives, but I want her back because living with a mentor is so much easier than living by faith.

My friend was to me what the law was to the Galatians–a mentor and a tutor whose purpose was to guide others toward faith in God. But we are not capable of possessing faith if we are still under the guidance of a tutor. At some point, we have to follow God on our own.

Here in Week Three we've been focusing on the subject of doubt. In Day One we recognized how the enemy uses doubt to cause us to question the truth. In Day Two we learned how Abraham, the father of our faith, dispelled doubt by driving it away and protecting the promises of God in his life. In Day Three we learned how to protect the promise of our salvation from doubt. And now in Day Four, we discover that the remedy for doubt is faith–not faith in the law or a mentor or a process that was meant to lead us to God, but faith in God alone.

The greatest antidote for doubt is faith. Every day, when doubt assails me and I long to hear my friends' validation, I am reminded of Peter who stepped out of the boat in Matthew 14:22–33, and whose only hope of walking on water was to look to Christ. When Paul wrote Galatians, he gave his audience the opportunity to place their faith in Christ and figuratively walk on water.

Read Matthew 14:27–29. Was anyone walking beside Peter when he got out of the boat?

True faith in Christ is a journey we embark upon alone. No one can do it for us. Fortunately, in John 16:13, Christ promised to give us an internal guide during our walk of faith toward him. Our guide, the Holy Spirit, is responsible to lead us into all truth. All we need to do is rest in that promise and step out in faith.

I would feel so much more secure if I still had my friend to lean on, but I'd never walk on water. Faith does have its advantages. It's not easy, but if we refuse to succumb to doubt and step out of the boat, then we'll go places with God that we never dreamed possible.

Prayer—*Lord, I hardly feel adequate to teach others how to overcome doubt, when I myself am constantly plagued with it. But the more I follow you in faith, the more I realize faith is not stepping out without doubt; it's stepping out in spite of it.*

Day 5: The Truth about Self-Doubt

Read Galatians 3:26–29.

In an interview with the *Dallas Observer,* Chris Martin described himself and others in his profession as a mixture of "enormous arrogance and terrible self-doubt."[6] Doubt, especially self-doubt, has a

6. Zac Crain, "Blood Work," *Dallas Observer,* August 22, 2002, http://www.dallasobserver.com/issues/2002-08-22/music.html.

way of identifying us. Christ's half-brother, the apostle James, writes in his epistle a description of a doubtful person.

Read James 1:6–8. What characteristics identify a doubtful person?

James' metaphor of a doubtful person being tossed by the wind is reminiscent of Peter's walk on the water in Matthew 14:30.

According to this verse, what did Peter see that made him afraid?

What did Christ do in Matthew 14:31, and what did he ask Peter?

When we step out to follow Christ in faith, doubt will assail us. It will attack us from all sides, just as the wind does the waves of the sea. Sometimes it will come in the form of others' opinions or in the form of circumstances that cause us uncertainty, but it will come to distract us from our destination.

When Peter saw the wind, he was distracted from his destination. He took his eyes off of Christ and focused on his circumstance. The first step in overcoming doubt in our lives is to remember whom we are walking toward. Never forget that the God we are walking toward is bigger than our circumstance. Christ proved that when he reached out his hand and rescued Peter.

The second step to overcoming doubt is found in today's verses from Galatians. These verses offer us specific protection from self-doubt and give us some great truths to remember when being faced with pervasive doubtful sentiments.

Read Galatians 3:26. Through faith in Christ, who are we?

____

____

Read Galatians 3:27. If we have been baptized into Christ, then with what have we been clothed?

____

____

Read Galatians 3:28. What are we in Christ?

____

____

Read Galatians 3:29. If we belong to Christ, then what are we?

____

____

A relationship with God based on faith opens a whole new world for us. No longer are we mere mortals limited by our race or gender or social status. We become sons of God, clothed with Christ, so that when God looks at us, he doesn't see our sin; he sees Christ. We also become a part of the promise God made to Abraham centuries ago when he said he would bless the whole world through Abraham. We become a part of that promise, and, in a way, we also become part of the fulfillment of that promise.

These benefits center on our immortal identity: who we are to God, how he views us, and who we are in relation to other Christians. Faith in God gives us an immortal identity which reminds us of who we really are and enables us to overcome the self-doubt in our lives.

Perhaps the most significant part of our immortal identity is found in Galatians 3:26 when Paul declares that we are sons of God. Many times throughout the Bible, masculine terms were used to identify both male and female, but in Galatians 3:26, I wonder if Paul's reference to us as "sons of God" might have had an even greater significance. You see, in biblical times, the son of the family inherited the father's name as well as his possessions. The daughter of the family, just like today, married and assumed the identity of another.

Paul writes in Galatians 3:26 that we are all sons of God through faith in Christ, and because we are sons, we have an identity that will not change and an inheritance that cannot be altered. Since we do not possess our own identity, but rather God's identity, then to doubt ourselves is ultimately to doubt the one whose name we bear.

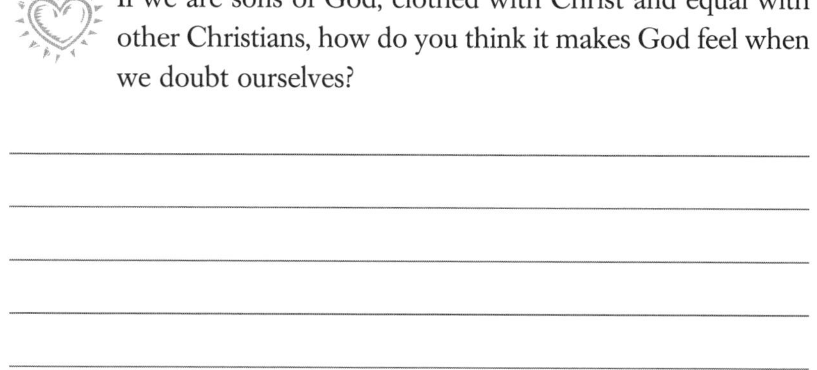

If we are sons of God, clothed with Christ and equal with other Christians, how do you think it makes God feel when we doubt ourselves?

Prayer–*I am your son, Lord. I bear your name and have full claim on all your possessions. And because of this, I can walk by faith. I refuse to allow self-doubt to cause me to question myself and my abilities, for to do that would really be to question you.*

BREAKAWAY FROM LEGALISM

Galatians Chapter 4

VOW: "Therefore, brothers, we are not children of the slave woman, but of the free woman."	Galatians 4:31

Day 1: Who's Your Daddy?

Read Galatians 4:1–5.

Little Timmy was a slave. He was a slave to his father's anger, serving as his punching bag when the fury was too much for his father to bear. Timmy's mother, Betty, would throw herself into the brawl in an attempt to protect her eldest child, but a grown man's wrath can be consuming, enslaving not only himself, but all those around him.

Timmy and his family were enslaved to their father's anger. Read Galatians 4:1–3. To what were the children of God enslaved?

Timmy's father, Horace Smith, was a truck driver and a slave to alcohol. As a result of his alcoholism, the Smith family became enslaved to the bouts of rage his drinking incited. It was a classic case of cause and effect. The alcohol was the cause; the abuse was the effect. The children of God were also enslaved, not necessarily to alcohol and subsequent abuse, but rather they succumbed to the principle of cause and effect. That is what Paul implies in verse 3 when he refers to the basic principles of this world. Our world is indeed governed by cause and effect. Even the laws of science concur. Newton's Third Law of Motion is commonly stated thus: "For every action there is an equal and opposite reaction."

The Law of Moses, given to the Jews during the Exodus, was based upon the law of cause and effect. If the Jews obeyed God's commandments, then God would bless them as they lived in the Promised Land. If they disobeyed God's commandments, God would punish them and banish them from the Promised Land. A short study of the Old Testament reveals that they did indeed disobey God's commandments; therefore, he exiled them to the pagan nations of Assyria and Babylon.

The Old Testament portrays the slavery of the children of God because the law of cause and effect governed God's relationship with his people. This led the Jews into the bondage of legalism. Legalism, which is defined as a strict adherence to a law or code of conduct, gives the illusion of spiritual maturity. In reality, it is an indication of one's spiritual immaturity. In the infancy stage of their relationship with the Lord, God allowed his children to be enslaved to legalism. But they were not destined to remain under legalism forever. At the appointed time, God's intent was to offer his people grace.

Grace overrode the law of cause and effect. It withheld from God's people the punishment their actions deserved and offered them forgiveness instead. It was the direct opposite of legalism.

God desired to offer grace to his people in order to emancipate them from their bondage of legalism. However, before he could give them grace, he first had to release them from the law they had initially agreed to follow in the Old Testament (see Exodus 19–31, 34). The key to their freedom lay in the offering of a perfect sacrifice, a sacrifice that had not sinned against the law, as they had. So in order to release them from the covenant they made with him, God had to offer a perfect sacrifice on their behalf.

Read Galatians 4:4, 5 and explain how God freed his people from legalism.

God sent his Son as the perfect sacrifice to free the Jews and all mankind from a relationship with him based on cause and effect. No longer would we have to wallow in a state of spiritual infancy. When Christ came, God allowed us a mature relationship with him based on his grace.

According to verse 5, what was another reason God sent his son to redeem us?

In 1977, when Timmy was ten years old, his mother and father divorced. No longer was he a slave to his father's rage, but he was still destined to live forever as the son of an abusive drunk. For God, it was not enough to remove us from the slavery of legalism; he desired to adopt us, make us his sons, and give us the full rights of sons.

Read John 8:35. Why do you think God wanted to make us his sons?

____

____

Timmy spent the first eleven years of his life believing he would forever belong to Horace Smith. But in 1978, Timmy was looking through some old pictures and files when he ran across his birth certificate, a document that would forever change the way he viewed himself. There, on his birth certificate under the title of father, was not the name, "Horace Smith, truck driver," but rather the name "Tug McGraw, professional baseball player"–the same Tug McGraw whose baseball card hung on Timmy's wall. In a state of disbelief, he confronted his mother, and she verified the truth: Tug McGraw, star pitcher for the Philadelphia Phillies, was Timmy's real father.

Timmy, known by fans as Tim McGraw, lived the first decade of his life in slavery under a guardian who was not even his father. But when the appropriate time came, his mother took her children and fled from Horace Smith. No longer a slave, Tim McGraw became a son. Not the son of an abusive drunk, but the son of a baseball legend.

Even though Tim McGraw's story is an inspirational one, it's still based upon the basic principles of this world. His paternity was based on cause and effect. The cause was a summer romance in 1966 between Tim's mother, Betty Trimble, and Tug McGraw. The two met in Jacksonville, Florida, while Tug was pitching for the minor league Jacksonville Suns. After a few dates, Tim was conceived; Tug was called back up to the majors to play for the Mets; and Betty fled home to her parents' house in Louisiana.

Tim's paternity was based on his parents' cause and effect, but it had nothing to do with his actions. Such is the case with our paternity. God caused his Son to redeem us from the law and the effect of that one act of redemption was that we were adopted as sons into the family of God, forever. Our paternity is based upon God's actions, not ours. If it had been based upon our actions, we would have remained slaves forever–constantly feeling that in order to become sons of God, we first had to do something to earn it.

Read Romans 8:15. What can enslave us?

A relationship with God based upon legalism is motivated by fear. Not a healthy, respectful fear of God, but rather a fear of God's wrath. In order to alleviate our fear, God made us his sons, independent of our actions. What a loving Father we have! A God who initiates a relationship with us, independent of the law of cause and effect, deserves a relationship from us without the fear of cause and effect.

Think about your relationship with the Lord; does legalism (or the law of cause and effect) play a role in your relationship with him? If so, how?

Prayer—*Lord, it's my nature to allow my life to be dictated by cause and effect. Help me realize those rules do not apply to my relationship with you. Your love and acceptance are not based upon such elemental things.*

Day 2: "He Calls Me 'Dad' "

Read Galatians 4:6–11.

At the age of eleven, little Timmy handled the news of his father's identity surprisingly well. He of course wanted to meet his baseball hero/father, but he didn't have unrealistic expectations of the man. He didn't request a private jet to fly him from his hometown in Start, Louisiana, to the city of brotherly love in order to take in a Phillies game with Tug and his wife and two children. All he wanted was to meet his father.

In response to Tim's appeal, his mother, Betty, called Tug after a decade of estrangement to request a meeting. Tug McGraw records their conversation in his book, *Ya Gotta Believe!* Unfortunately for Tim, when Betty told Tug he was the father, Tug didn't believe it and requested Betty quit referring to him as Tim's dad.

In Galatians 4:6, 7, Paul told the Galatians God had made them sons. According to verse 6, what had God given the Galatians, and what did his gift enable his sons to do?

____

____

____

On January 7, 2004, two days after his father's death, Tim McGraw wrote the introduction to his father's book, *Ya Gotta Believe!,* and in his introduction he wrote these words: "I am his son, but I never called him Dad."[1] It isn't enough for God to just make us his sons; he wants us to call him "Dad." So our Father sent the Spirit of his Son into our hearts. And his Spirit within us refers to God as "Abba, Father." The word *Abba* is an Aramaic word used as a term of endearment for one's father. It is a term of affection equivalent to our word "Dad."

Have you ever called God "Dad"?

In Galatians 4:1–5, the apostle Paul established the fact that the Galatians had been freed from slavery and given a wonderful Father. In verses 6 and 7, he established that the Galatians had been given permission to call their father "Dad." Now, in verses 8–11 of this chapter, Paul goes on to describe how the Galatians reacted to all these privileges.

Read Galatians 4:8–11. According to these verses, had they accepted these privileges?

---

1. Tug McGraw, *Ya Gotta Believe!* (New York, New American Library, 2004), introduction.

Little Tim eventually got his meeting with his father. It occurred in Houston when the Phillies were in town to play the Houston Astros. But if Tim was looking for a father, he failed to find one during that first rendezvous. Still unable to accept the possibility that Tim was his biological son, Tug suggested that Tim refer to him as his buddy. A buddy is a far cry from a dad, but Tim left his visit with renewed hope and changed his last name from Smith to McGraw.

A year later when Tim was twelve, he requested another visit with Tug. They agreed to meet, once again at the Astrodome in Houston while the Phillies were in town. When Tim's mother brought him down to the dugout to arrange a time for Tug and Tim to meet privately, Tug declined her offer and consequently broke his son's heart. After that trip, Tim went home and changed his name back to Smith and made no attempts to contact Tug for many years.

Tim had good reason to deny his father, but the Galatians' only reason for denying their Abba Father was their preference for the weak and miserable principles of the world. In other words, they preferred a relationship with God based on cause and effect instead of a father/son relationship.

What are some ways we can choose to have a legalistic, cause and effect relationship with God instead of a father/son relationship?

____

____

____

____

____

____

____

I've tried to have a relationship with God based on cause and effect. And surprisingly enough, the time I was most prone to fall into that type of relationship was when my husband and I were in full-time ministry. Let's face it; the ministry is not exactly a lucrative profession. There's sacrifice involved. We didn't live like paupers, but we were most definitely denied the comforts of wealth. I remember thinking that such piety and sacrifice on my part certainly merited an occasional favor or two from the Almighty. And I convinced myself that all my sacrifice on God's behalf made him obligated to me. My good works were the cause, and the effect should have been God's blessings.

Needless to say, God did not give me what I wanted when I made such selfish requests of him. And of course, like every selfish child, I would get angry at him. Sometimes that selfish anger can make a son want to change his last name like Tim McGraw did after his father disappointed him. At the very least, our anger inhibits our ability to call God "Dad."

But this is the very type of dysfunctional relationship God freed us from in Galatians 4. No longer are we mandated to do certain things to gain our Father's approval and blessing. But by the same token, no longer are we able to believe we can manipulate our Father by our good works.

I think that is the real reason the Galatians went back to a legalistic, cause and effect relationship with the Father. It wasn't that they didn't want to be sons; I think it was because they didn't want to relinquish control of the relationship. Too bad they didn't realize they never really had any control to begin with.

I suppose at some point, as sons of God, we all must come to the understanding that we have absolutely no control over our Father. Because he is our Father, he is the one in control of our relationship and our lives. This is a hard truth to accept, but to make it a little easier, God sent the Spirit of his Son Jesus into our hearts, and Christ's Spirit within us cries out, "Abba, Father," or "Dad."

There is one instance in scripture when Jesus calls God "Abba, Father." The circumstances surrounding Christ's outcry are rather dismal, but the words Christ utters to God reveal what it really means when God's sons call him "Dad."

Write Christ's words in Mark 14:36 below.

___

___

___

When we call God "Dad" we relinquish control of our lives. We admit that in every circumstance, our Father knows best. We surrender.

Earlier in this lesson, I asked if you have ever called God "Dad." After learning what it truly means to call him "Dad," do you still wish to refer to him in such a way? And if so, why?

___

___

___

Prayer–*Abba Daddy, while I think I'm the most blessed person in the world to have you for a father, I'm still painfully aware of my humanity. I can be willful and belligerent at times, completely distracted by this world and the things in it. And surrender is difficult for me. So when I call you "Dad," I want you to know that this term and all it implies does not come easy. But from the depths of my soul, I mean it.*

Day 3: Sibling Rivalry

Read Galatians 4:12–20.

In Galatians 4, Paul pleads with the Galatians to realize the family they are forsaking when they rely upon a legalistic, cause and effect relationship with God. Not only are they forsaking their Father and the opportunity to call him "Dad," but they are also forsaking other members of their family.

Read Galatians 4:12–14. How does Paul refer to the Galatians in verse 12?

____

____

How did the Galatians treat their brother, Paul, during his first visit with them?

____

____

Read Galatians 4:15, 16. According to verse 16, what has Paul now become to them?

____

____

Sometimes it is easy to believe our relationship with the Lord is exclusive only to us, but because our entrance into the kingdom welcomes us into a family of believers, our actions affect others. The Galatians' actions were having a devastating effect on Paul. Not only did God feel betrayed by their decision to revert back to the law, Paul felt betrayed as well.

Have you ever grieved over a believer's decision to turn his or her back on God?

____

____

____

____

One of the reasons Tug McGraw gave for initially denying his son's attempts at a relationship was the fact that Tug already had a wife and two kids at home. At the time of Tim's first phone call, Tug's children, Mark and Cari, were six and four. To introduce a new sibling into an already established household would have only added pain and confusion, so Tug opted not to do it.

It took Tug over six years to make that introduction, and just as long to make the confession. While driving down to Florida to meet seventeen-year-old Tim for a family vacation, Tug finally told his children they had an older brother. Much to his surprise, they were very accepting of their older sibling.

Unfortunately, the Galatians were also accepting of people, but not their siblings in Christ. Paul's rebuke of them in Galatians 4 proves the Galatians had accepted some real scoundrels into their lives.

Read Galatians 4:17. Describe the motives of the people the Galatians had come to accept.

____

____

In today's passage of scripture, Paul gives us three indicators to determine whether or not we are being controlled by legalism. All of these indicators describe the Galatians' actions while under the control of the Judaizers' teachings.

Read Galatians 4:15. What did Paul ask the Galatians in this verse?

The first indicator of a life controlled by legalism is a loss of joy. While the New International Vesion translates the Greek *makarismos* in verse 15 as "joy," the New American Standard Bible translates *makarismos* as "a sense of blessing." In other words, the Galatians had once pronounced blessings upon their brother Paul and had been filled with joy in his presence. But while under the control of legalism, the Galatians no longer enjoyed the fellowship of their brother in Christ.

Legalism is exclusive. It separates us from other Christians who do not believe as we do. It causes us to question their salvation because their lives are not dictated by the same standards of holiness we hold ourselves to. Some people get legalistic over church attendance or wearing certain clothes or abstaining from alcohol. Such people believe that these outward displays of piety make them more righteous, when in reality, these pious acts rob them of their joy and separate them from other believers.

What was Paul's question in Galatians 4:16?

The second indicator of legalism is an inability to receive the truth. Paul spoke truth to the Galatians, but they were unwilling to receive that truth. Not only did they fail to receive the truth, they were so hostile against it that they viewed their brother in Christ as an enemy.

Paul was not the only follower of God viewed as an enemy. Jesus Christ, God's only begotten son, was also labeled as an adversary. Among his many accusers were the Pharisees, a group of Jewish religious leaders. They opposed Christ's message because they were blinded by legalism. The Pharisees were so deceived by their own piety that they rejected Jesus, who not only spoke the truth, but, according to John 14:6, *was* the truth.

According to verse 17, what did the Judaizers want to do to the Galatians?

___

___

___

The third and final indicator of a life controlled by legalism is alienation. The enemy will always try to alienate us from our heavenly family. In fact, all three of these indicators manage to separate us from our brothers and sisters in Christ. Perhaps it is because the enemy knows that if we are alienated from other believers, we will be easier to control. But I also wonder if there is another reason legalism makes us feel alienated.

Today, Tug's eldest son, Tim, is the most popular male performer in country music. His marriage to country star Faith Hill has further solidified his fame while his multi-platinum albums and slew of music awards have made him a living legend. The siblings he met in Florida many years ago have gone on to live rather quiet lives. Half-brother Mark is a fireman/EMT in Oregon; half-sister Cari owns a coffee shop in California.

How would you feel if you were Mark or Cari?

___

___

You see, when we are controlled by legalism, we base our relationship with God on our abilities. When that is the case, anyone with superior abilities becomes a threat to us, even if they are our siblings in Christ. We oftentimes alienate ourselves from them because we are jealous of them.

Have you ever been jealous of another brother or sister in Christ? Why do you think Christians often become jealous of other Christians?

____

____

____

____

____

Prayer–*Abba, Daddy, I must admit I have been jealous of my siblings in Christ. Sometimes I'm jealous because they are more gifted than I am, and other times I'm jealous because I wonder if you like them more than you like me. Maybe they're more holy or more spiritually mature, and surely you would prefer their company over mine. I know these emotions are rooted in legalism and insecurity, and your love is not based on such bondage. But I pray that whenever I am tempted to feel this way, you would remind me of who I am to you–not who I am compared to my other siblings in Christ, but who I am to you.*

Day 4: A Matter of Maternity

Read Galatians 4:21–27.

Tug McGraw and his son, Tim, grew up under the guidance of two completely different women. Tug's mother, Mabel, suffered from manic depression and sought solace at the Napa State Mental Hospital. Her stays at the hospital meant Tug and his brother, Hank, would be granted brief reprieves from their mother's physical abuse.

Complete the chart below using the information Paul gives in Galatians 4:21–23. (Refer to Genesis 21:1–10 to discover the names of the birth mothers.)

Abraham's Sons	Description of Birth Mother	Born According to What?
Son # 1 – Ishmael		
Son # 2 – Isaac		

In yet another attempt to convince the Galatians of their freedom in Christ, Paul offers them an example from the Old Testament. Since the Judaizers were so accustomed to claiming Abraham as their father, Paul thought it pertinent to remind them of Abraham's situation. The Jews often mistakenly believed their salvation was guaranteed because they had Abraham as their ancestor and thus to enjoy the benefits of a relationship with God, one either had to be born a Jew or convert to Judaism (which meant following the law). In this passage, Paul reminds both Jews and Gentiles that Abraham fathered two children. One child was born in the ordinary way and was the result of willful determination; the other was born in accordance with a promise and was the result of faith.

Paul takes his allegory one step further in Galatians 4:24. Fill in the blank below.

"These things may be taken figuratively, for the women represent two ____________."

Read Galatians 4:24–26. Can you decipher what each woman's covenant represents?

____

____

____

Because Mount Sinai was the location where Moses received the law, it marked the origin of the Jew's slavery to the law. At the time Paul wrote Galatians, the Jews living in Jerusalem were still attempting to worship God in accordance with the law. For this reason, Paul correlated the city of Jerusalem with Mount Sinai and then took it one step further by correlating them both with slavery.

In Paul's illustration, Abraham represents the Lord, while the two women represent two different covenants. Hagar represents the temporary covenant of slavery, which is the law. Sarah represents the eternal covenant of freedom, which we receive through faith in Jesus Christ. Paul cites her city of reference as the Jerusalem that is from above, meaning it is a spiritual realm–not something that can be attained in the flesh or by the law.

According to Paul's allegory, the Galatians needed to choose a mother to follow. If they chose to live by legalism, which results in slavery, then who would be their mother?

____

____

If they chose to live by faith and freedom, then whom would they be able to claim as their mother?

Mabel's maternal influence was difficult for Tug to overcome. He spent a great deal of his life struggling to be the husband and father his family deserved. Life on the road as a professional baseball player offered him many female temptations, most of which he found too difficult to resist. His famous quote regarding his money was, "Ninety percent, I'll spend on good times, women and Irish whiskey. The other 10 percent, I'll probably waste."[2]

Tug's words of revelry are in stark contrast to the life his son has chosen to lead. Despite a host of female fans and *People* magazine's title of "Sexiest Country Star," Tim McGraw maintains a family-man image. His wife of nine years, Faith Hill, and three daughters, Gracie, Maggie, and Audrey receive the full force of his affections. When asked about his wife, Tim told *Parade* magazine, "I had fun for a long time as a bachelor, but when Faith came along, all of that changed. She holds my soul in her heart. She's everything."[3] His commitment to his daughters runs just as deep. Concern for their welfare made him promise to scale back his work if necessary, stating, "It's not a sacrifice at all. It's all about family."[4]

In *Ya Gotta Believe!*, Tug McGraw describes his eldest son as being a better man than any of the other men in his (Tim's) life. In the book, Tug admires Tim's commitment to his family and his determination to provide his children with an advantage Tim never had–a dedicated father. Tug credits Tim's success to Tim's mom,

2. "The One and Only," *The Morning Call* (Allentown, PA), January 8, 2004.
3. Ben Fong-Torres, "It's All Family Now," *Parade*, August 22, 2004, http://archive.parade.com/2004/0822/0822_tim_mcgraw.html.
4. Ibid.

Betty, whom Tug describes as a great mother who did an incredible job raising his son.[5]

Two sons raised by two vastly different women went on to become two vastly different men. As sons of God, we are given the opportunity to determine the mother who will raise us. We can either be sons of slavery raised under the guidance of legalism, forever trying to be righteous by our own merit. Or, we can choose to be sons of freedom, whose only claim to righteousness lies in our faith in Jesus Christ. One mother will make our relationship with the Lord an obligation; the other will make it a privilege. One mother will control us by feelings of guilt and shame; the other will free us through forgiveness and grace. But whatever mother we choose will determine the kind of son we will be for our Dad.

Which mother have you chosen and how has that decision affected your relationship with your Father?

5. McGraw, *Ya Gotta Believe!*, 172.

Prayer–*Abba, Father, whenever I feel shame and guilt I know I have chosen slavery as my maternal influence. Sometimes those feelings are so familiar to me that I mistakenly believe they are from you. Thank you that they are not, and that my true destiny is to live under the maternal influence of freedom.*

Day 5: Live Like You Were Dying

Read Galatians 4:28–31.

Days One and Two of this week's lesson were spent examining how legalism and the law of cause and effect can influence our relationship with our Abba Father. In Day Three of our study, we learned how a legalistic mindset can affect our relationship with our siblings in Christ. In Day Four, we were given the illustration of motherhood. One mother represents slavery to legalism, and the other mother represents freedom through faith. Here in Day Five we will see that Paul concludes Galatians 4 with yet another analogy of family.

How does Paul address the Galatians in verse 28?

____

____

____

In what way does he compare them to Isaac?

____

____

In verse 29, what does the slave woman's son do to the free woman's son?

____

____

____

____

According to verse 30, what should be done to the slave woman and her son?

____

____

____

____

In March 2003, at the age of fifty-eight, Tug McGraw was working at the Phillies' spring training camp in Clearwater, Florida, when he began to experience erratic speech patterns and loss of muscle control. On the morning of March 12th, he experienced symptoms which led him to believe he was having a stroke. After being rushed to the hospital, doctors ordered an MRI that revealed two masses in his head–brain cancer.

The attending physician thought it best to be very direct with the baseball legend. After first breaking the news to Tug, he later addressed the family. His predictions were grim. He gave the former left-handed pitcher a death sentence–three weeks was all the time he had left. Upon hearing news of his father's prognosis, Tim McGraw uttered two life-changing words: "That's unacceptable."[6]

6. McGraw, *Ya Gotta Believe!*, 8.

Some things in life are just "unacceptable." The apostle Paul thought so. He makes it very clear in our Day Five scripture passage that it is unacceptable for those people bound by legalism to persecute those who live by faith in Christ. In fact, he goes so far as to tell Christians (the children of promise) to purge themselves from the influence of those persons bound by legalism.

In order to fight for his life, Tug McGraw had to rid himself of the death sentence the neurosurgeon had pronounced over him. With the help of his son, Tim, he was moved to a hospital that specialized in his aggressive form of brain cancer. His transfer allowed him to meet another surgeon who agreed to perform surgery to remove the tumors.

What declaration does Paul make in Galatians 4:31?

____

____

____

After a successful surgery, Tug's doctor, a longtime fan, offered the family encouragement by repeating a declaration Tug had coined during his 1973 season with the New York Mets: "Ya Gotta Believe." More than anything, the apostle Paul longed for the Galatians to truly believe they were sons of the free woman, born by the Spirit and emancipated from legalism and the law of cause and effect. They no longer needed to accept persecution from the Judaizers who were confusing them in their faith. Nor did they need to remain enslaved to guilt and shame. So in order to protect their freedom and their faith, they had to liberate themselves from any thoughts or outside influences that limited their spiritual liberty.

Think about your life; are there any influences that limit your spiritual liberty? If so, what are they?

____

____

____

____

____

I have noticed in my own life that I cannot be close to fearful people. I can love them and try to minister to them, but I can never allow them to become my close, personal friends. You see, fear is contagious. And if I surround myself with fearful people, then I'll allow their fears to become my fears. I cannot do that, because fear always stifles my spiritual freedom.

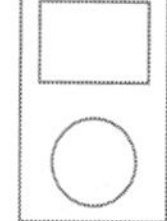

Interact with Your iPod®

Download Tim McGraw's song "Live Like You Were Dying."

- Do you think the man in this song was truly free from the fear of cause and effect?
- Was his life richer because of his freedom?

When we live legalistic lives, our actions are dictated by fear. Fear is the motivating force behind the law of cause and effect. And a desire for control is the motivating force behind fear. Fear is a symptom of control. Our fears are dictated by our desire to control our lives; we will fear whatever threatens our control. The man in Tim McGraw's song should fear his disease, because it threatens his control over his life. However, instead, he enjoys a life of freedom, because he realizes he is no longer in control of his life; his disease is. Instead of fighting his disease and trying to maintain an illusion of control, he lets go, embraces the freedom his disease offers, and lives life as though he were dying.

Read Galatians 2:19, 20. Why should we as Christians live like we are dying?

____

____

The truth is, as Christians, we aren't just dying; we're already dead. We're dead to legalism. We're dead to fear and the illusion of control it gives. We relinquished control of our lives the moment we accepted Christ as our Lord and Savior. We died, and he now lives within us. His Spirit is controlling us, dictating our actions and our freedom.

Recognizing our lack of control allows us to live like Paul lived, as described in Galatians 2:20, "by faith in the Son of God." Freedom in Christ is motivated by faith. Fear and legalism are motivated by our attempts to maintain control of our lives. Our fight for control keeps us in bondage. But faith liberates us to live life to the fullest, both spiritually and otherwise.

Review Day Two of this week.

Can you recall what it means to call God "Dad"?

____

____

When we relinquish control of our lives, what are we actually saying to our Abba Daddy?

Because of great medical care, Tug McGraw's life was extended nine months beyond the original prognosis of three weeks. During this time he wrote his autobiography and made memories with his children, especially youngest son, Matthew, who was seven at the time. He completely relinquished control of his life on January 5, 2004, when he died in Tim McGraw's Tennessee home. Not long after, Tim released the song "Live Like You Were Dying," which fans recognized as a tribute to his father.

The best tribute we as sons can give our heavenly Father is to live our short lives here on earth as though we were dying–enjoying our spiritual freedom by relinquishing control of our lives and crying, "Abba, Daddy, you truly do know what is best for my life, so have your way."

Prayer–*Abba Father, I never realized how my attempts at maintaining control of my life actually enslave me. I don't want to remain in bondage to my will and my need to control. I want to enjoy the life of freedom your Spirit provides. Allow me to embrace your freedom and live every day in anticipation of spending eternity with you. I have only a limited amount of time here on earth, and God, I want it to mean something. I want my life to be a tribute to you, so let me live each day surrendered to you.*

BREAKAWAY TO FREEDOM

Galatians Chapter 5

VOW: "It is for freedom that Christ has set us free. Stand firm, then, and do not let yourselves be burdened by a yoke of slavery."	Galatians 5:1

Day 1: I Still Haven't Found What I'm Looking For

Read Galatians 5:1

I suppose most professional writers call it "writer's block." To me, it feels more like a "Spirit stop." The Irish band, U2, wrote a song about it entitled "I Still Haven't Found What I'm Looking For." No matter how you describe it, there is still no getting around mankind's lack of answers.

As a writer, I want answers to Galatians 5. I want to know what freedom in Christ really is. I want points by which to model my life. But while attempting to write this week's concentration of study, I was met with more questions than answers–leading to a severe case of writer's block. And yet, it was more than writer's block. For quite some time, I didn't feel I had God's permission to write this lesson–thus the "Spirit stop." And though eventually I felt his permission to write, I struggled as to how I should approach this subject of freedom. I'm still searching for the true meaning of freedom. In other words, I still haven't found what I'm looking for.

I could go the more religious route and pretend I'm living so much by faith that I'm confident Christ's work on the cross will give me every answer I need for every question I encounter in life–that the bondages I see in my life and in the lives of others can be alleviated with one quick-fix solution. And I could operate under the assumption that every quick-fix solution I need can be found in the Bible, if I just look hard enough. And in finding these quick-fix solutions, not only will I become more acquainted with the God who is all-knowing, but I too might also be able to attain to some level of omniscience myself.

Write Galatians 5:1 below.

____

____

In the first two chapters of Galatians, Paul defends his gospel from legalism. In our study of chapters 3 and 4, we have seen Paul make his case against legalism, and now, as we move into chapter 5, we discover Paul presenting closing arguments regarding legalism. Simply put, he tells the Galatians they are free. But he gives them two directives needed to maintain their freedom.

Study Galatians 5:1. Can you find the two commands Paul gives the Galatians to assist them in protecting their freedom?

____

____

These are rather vague directives in my opinion. I would have preferred Paul write out a detailed analysis to secure our freedom, something akin to the Pentagon's plan for executing Operation Iraqi Freedom. It may have been a plan fraught with adversity, but at least it would have made me feel as though I had some answers. However, Paul wasn't really interested in giving answers. He was more interested in securing freedom for the Galatians–a freedom they had apparently enjoyed prior to their acquaintance with the Judaizers. So in the midst of their freedom fight, the only instructions Paul gave the Galatians were to stand firm and to not allow themselves to be burdened by another yoke of slavery.

On what were they to stand firm?

____

____

____

How would they be able to recognize another yoke of slavery when it came their way?

____

____

____

I don't have the answers to these questions, but maybe you do. I can make educated guesses. Maybe the Galatians were supposed to stand on their faith that they were saved by grace and not by legalism. Maybe they could recognize a yoke of slavery by comparing it to the one they were currently under. Maybe those are the right answers to these questions. Maybe they're not.

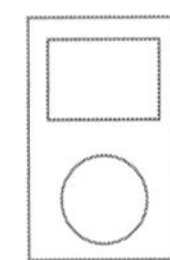

Interact with Your iPod®

Download U2's 1987 hit song "I Still Haven't Found What I'm Looking For."

- Do you recognize the references to Christ in this song?
- Has your relationship with Christ enabled you to find every answer you've been looking for?

When U2 released their fifth album, *The Joshua Tree,* they received a lot of criticism from the Christian community. Since three of the four members of the U2 band had claimed to be Christians, their song left some in the religious community outraged. To blatantly admit that faith in Christ did not come with a pre-packaged set of answers to all life's problems was blasphemy to some. Bono, The Edge, and Larry Mullen may have believed that God sent his Son to die for mankind's sins, but their belief in Christ did not offer them answers to all their hearts' longings. They knew there was more–more to look for, more solutions to be sought, more questions to be answered.

One of the key components of legalism is the need to have all the answers–to reproduce God's all-knowing nature here on earth (an attribute we as Christians have never been promised). God forbid we ever find what we're looking for and suddenly know all the answers, because that would make us gods.

I've struggled a lot trying to come up with some answer to assist me in my own fight for freedom. And the only thing God has shown me is that legalism not only strives for control, it also strives to be all-knowing, to possess all the answers, or at least pretend to.

As a Christian, have you ever felt the need to pretend your faith in Christ gives you the answers to all of life's questions? If so, give an example.

____

____

____

____

____

____

____

____

____

"At one time, I thought you had to have all the answers if you were going to write a song, so it was embarrassing to make a record that was filled with doubts and questions. Then I began to see that many of the artists who inspire me. . . . had similar feelings of awkwardness and spiritual confusion. I realize now its OK to say you still haven't found what you're searching for." - Bono[1]

A few years ago I was at a Christian concert, and I listened as the band changed the words of U2's song to make them more politically correct for a Christian audience. Their lyrics, "I finally found what I'm looking for," still echo in my ears. At the time, I thought them incredibly enlightening. Now, I feel they're fraudulent. Yes, Christ has filled the God-shaped hole in my heart. But my salvation did not come with a guaranteed solution to all of life's problems. I still struggle and question and strive for answers that never come.

And perhaps that is the essence of freedom in Christ. To no longer

1. Robert Hillman, "At Home in Dublin," *Los Angeles Times,* April 12, 1987.

have to pretend that things are okay when they are not. To no longer pretend we possess the answers to all life's problems. To be honest with ourselves and admit that we too search and strive for answers that may never come. To realize that the God we serve is all knowing, but we are not. And to confess that our relationship with him does not guarantee us a solution to all our problems.

> ". . . a certain honesty with yourself . . . that's what sets you free." - Bono[2]

I stand firm in that awareness. And I am now able to recognize the yoke of legalism when it is cloaked in a need to have all the answers and possess all the solutions. Knowing all the answers is not faith. We were called to walk, not just in freedom, but in faith. I think the two go hand in hand.

Have you ever considered that a need to have all the answers is a form of legalism?

____

____

____

____

What are some ways we can breakaway from this form of legalism?

____

____

____

____

2. Michka Assaya, *Bono In Conversation* (New York: Riverhead Books, 2005), 128–129.

Prayer—*Lord, thank you that I don't have to pretend to have all the answers. Thank you for the freedom to question and search and admit that in some instances, I still haven't found what I'm looking for. Thank you that it is often in my search for answers that I encounter you. I may not always get the answers to my questions, but I always get you. And that, Lord, is true freedom.*

Day 2: I Thought I Found What I Was Looking For

Read Galatians 5:2–6

According to Galatians 5:2, Christ would no longer be of any value to the Galatians if they did what?

___

___

___

The Galatians thought they had the Christian life figured out. They thought it could be boiled down to a few "dos" and "don'ts." When they found the law, they thought they'd finally found what they were looking for. They thought a set of laws could replace a relationship with God and still, somehow, please him. And their erroneous mindset was signified by their willingness to be circumcised.

Read Galatians 5:3. What was expected of every man who was circumcised?

___

___

Circumcision represented one's commitment to follow the whole law. Paul wanted the Galatians to know that circumcision bound them to the law. And the law made them slaves.

According to Galatians 5:4, what else did the law do to those who were trying to be justified by it?

A few years ago, a friend gave me a book about the spiritual origins of various diseases. It had a lot of good insights in it. It made me feel wise and discerning. It revealed how certain sins could manifest themselves in the form of certain illnesses and that one could experience physical healing, and even eradicate all future illness, simply through confessing sin.

I thought I had found every answer to mankind's medical questions. I thought I'd finally found what I was looking for. I could avoid life's illnesses and walk pain-free throughout life. And all I had to do to achieve this goal was to remain sin-free.

I realize now this flawed belief system was my attempt to be justified by the law. I attempted to work out my own life according to my righteousness. I wanted to please God and subsequently avoid sickness through my own perfection. But in reality, my attempts alienated me from Christ. They caused me to fall from grace–not the grace by which I am saved, but the grace by which I enjoy a loving, growing relationship with the Lord.

Grace is God's gift of unconditional love and acceptance of us. Whenever we, as believers, try to appease God (or manipulate him, which I tried to do) by our good works, then we refuse to accept God's gift. We place conditions of righteousness on our relationship that God never intended. He doesn't want our righteousness, just our faith in him that he will one day make us righteous.

Write Galatians 5:5 below.

____

____

____

____

Legalism misleads us into believing we can attain our own righteousness. Faith enables us to wait for the righteousness that only God can give. Therefore, faith makes us dependent upon God. I don't like being dependent. Perhaps that's why I'm so tempted by legalism, because it gives me a sense of control, a sense of independence. The Galatians craved independence. They thought they had finally found what they had been looking for when they found legalism and circumcision. But Paul told them none of that mattered.

According to Galatians 5:6, what is the only thing that really matters?

____

____

____

____

I thought I had finally found what I'd been looking for when I read my friend's book about diseases. I had all the answers to my medical questions, all the remedies for life's ailments. But what I did not have was love.

After months and months of immersing myself in the teachings found in that book, I began to recognize a lack of love in my life. No longer was I extending love and compassion to those who were sick and hurting, because I was too busy condemning them for their sin. Finally I told my friend that I couldn't read her book anymore, because I didn't like the effect it was having on me.

Have you ever followed a teaching or a system of beliefs that resulted in a lack of love in your life? If so, explain.

____

____

____

____

____

____

____

Legalism is insidious. It creeps into our core beliefs under the guise of truth. It weaves its way into our thoughts and feelings until we convince ourselves it is truth. And in the end, it leaves us devoid of love. Legalism comes in many different forms, but its end result is always the same. It always ends in a loss of love. Sometimes legalism causes us to lose our love for others; sometimes it causes us to lose our love for ourselves; and other times, it causes us to lose our love for God.

Paul wanted to protect the Galatians from legalism. He knew that legalism could never coexist with faith and love. So he told them that the only thing that really mattered was faith expressing itself through love. If faith and love are evident in your life, then be encouraged my friend, because legalism has no hold on you.

Prayer—*Lord, had you not revealed to me the lack of love in my life, I might have never recognized the legalistic mindset I had come to embrace. Thank you for revealing my legalism to me. Please fill my heart with faith and love so I'll no longer be deceived by legalism.*

Day 3: A Life of Faith

Read Galatians 5:7–12.

In September of 1974, Paul Hewson watched as his mother collapsed during his grandfather's funeral. Unfortunately, the brain hemorrhage Mrs. Hewson suffered at her father's funeral resulted in her own death. To cope with his grief, her fourteen-year-old son, Paul, sought solace in music and religion. But religion had torn his hometown of Dublin, Ireland, apart, segregating it into Protestant communities and Catholic communities. As the son of a Roman Catholic father and a Protestant mother, Paul knew firsthand the divisiveness of religion.

Read Galatians 5:7. What had happened to the Galatians?

___

___

___

Religion played a divisive role in the church at Galatia. This division did not separate the Galatians from each other, but rather it separated them from the truth. The Judaizers, with their rules and regulations, had imposed restrictions on these new believers that not only kept them from obeying the truth but also kept them from enjoying a relationship with the only one who was the Truth (see John 14:6).

What does Paul tell the Galatians in verse 8?

____

____

____

It's easy to be persuaded, especially when that persuasion comes from those we respect and is replete with notions of piety and righteousness. But any persuasion that steers us away from the truth is not from God, even if it comes from those we revere.

Paul speaks truth to the Galatians in Galatians 3:11. What is the truth found in this verse?

____

____

____

In 1976, young Paul Hewson discovered his love for music when he answered an ad on the bulletin board at school. The ad, posted by Larry Mullen, sought musicians interested in forming a new band. Eight musicians replied, but four lost interest, leaving only Paul Hewson (nicknamed "Bono"), Adam Clayton, Larry Mullen, and Dave Evans (nicknamed "The Edge"). After several attempts to identify themselves, the band discarded the names, "Feedback" and "The Hype," eventually settling on the name, "U2."

Not long after discovering their band's identity, three members of the band sought to reclaim their spiritual identity. They did this through the teachings of a Christian religious group in Dublin called Shalom. While growing spiritually, the band also began to expand commercially. They released their first album, *Boy*, in 1980, followed by their second album, *October*, in 1981. It was during the release of *October* that the band nearly called it quits.

Influenced by the piety of their Shalom fellowship and persuaded by their own inner voices of legalism, the three Christian members of U2 considered abandoning their pursuit of rock-and-roll greatness. Claiming they could no longer reconcile their religious beliefs with their chosen profession, Bono, The Edge, and Larry Mullen approached their manager, Paul McGuiness, to inform him they wanted out of the band.

Years later, in a 1988 interview with Liam Mackey of the Irish magazine *Hot Press*, Bono reflected on his encounter with legalism stating,

> Yeah, we were a bit uptight at one stage . . . when we first started exploring the teachings of Christ and studying the Scriptures, we got involved in something that on one level was opening our minds to a wider reality but which on another just closed us off to certain experiences. But you know you go through things.[3]

In some ways, the Galatian church encountered the same experience. As they grew in Christ and opened their minds to a wider reality of God, they also allowed the Judaizers to place restrictions on their faith that God never intended. Those restrictions, which included circumcision, would have inevitably closed them off and isolated them from others. God's Holy Spirit in their lives was what set them apart from others; therefore there was no need to be further set apart by undergoing circumcision.

After the Christian members of U2 informed Paul McGuiness of their decision, he convinced the band to remain intact until the com-

3. Liam Mackey, "I Still Haven't Found What I'm Looking For," *Hot Press*, December 1, 1988.

pletion of the worldwide *October* tour. Apparently, the tour proved to be just what the band needed, because after it, no other notions of disbanding were entertained.

In a 1995 book *U2 at the End of the World*, band member The Edge commented on the band's earlier dilemma,

> I suppose we've changed our attitudes a lot since then. The central faith and spirit of the band is the same. But I have less and less time for legalism now. I just see that you live a life of faith. It's nothing to do necessarily with what clothes you wear or whether you drink or smoke or who you're seeing or not seeing.[4]

Return to Galatians 3:11. How should the righteous live?

____

____

____

What do you think requires more faith–to live life according to a strict code of conduct surrounded by others with similar convictions **or** to live life by faith in Christ amid the temptations of this world? Explain your answer.

____

____

____

____

4. Bill Flanagan, *U2 at the End of the World* (New York: Bantam Doubleday Dell Publishing, 1995), 49.

I must be honest with you; this whole chapter is hard for me. I'm hesitant to promote a rock star band as a model for Christian living. Their lives are the complete antithesis of all I've ever been raised to believe as holy. Their drinking, smoking, and swearing leave me to wonder just how far this salvation by grace thing can go.

> "I wish I could live the life of someone you could describe as pious. I couldn't preach because I couldn't practice. It's plain to see I'm not a good advertisement for God."
>
> –Bono[5]

And yet, there is no denying their faith in God. In all I've researched, in all I've studied, in all the lyrics I've listened to, I'm completely convinced that there is substance to their faith. My difficulty lies in the fact that their faith does not look like my faith. And, perhaps, therein lies my own legalistic stumbling block.

Prayer–*Lord, I like living by a strict code of conduct because it makes me feel safe and secure. It convinces me that I'm giving you exactly what you want and that I'm pleasing you. It keeps me from encountering the pitfalls of sin. It isolates me, places me in a bubble, and keeps me from having to wade out into the murky waters of faith. I can see why the Galatians were so drawn to the Judaizers' message, because it seemed like the right thing to do. But your ways are higher than mine, Lord. And what seems right to me may in fact be the very thing that stifles my faith. So please, Father, give me the courage to get out of my bubble and allow you to guide me through these murky waters of faith, even when my faith walk differs from others.*

5. Assaya, 25.

Day 4: A Call to Freedom

Read Galatians 5:13–15

In his letter to the Galatians, the apostle Paul informs believers of two things that endanger their freedom. He spends four and a half chapters detailing the first inhibitor of freedom–legalism, yet he only spends fourteen verses expounding on the second inhibitor of freedom–the flesh.

For the remainder of this lesson, we will study Paul's second inhibitor of freedom, but before we do, why do you think Paul spent so much energy warning the Galatians against legalism and so little energy warning them against the flesh?

____

____

____

Both inhibitors, legalism and the flesh, are in direct opposition to each other. One imposes strict rules and regulations and errs on the side of caution, whereas the other imposes no rules or regulations and errs on the side of indulgence. True freedom in Christ is found somewhere in the middle of these two extremes.

Read Galatians 5:13.

To what were the Galatians called?

____

____

____

____

What were they not to use their freedom for?

____

____

____

Instead they were to use their freedom to do what?

____

____

____

U2 recognized their call to freedom in the early 1980s when they divested themselves of the legalistic mindset that almost destroyed their destinies. But liberty from legalism could have easily caused them to use their freedom to indulge the sinful nature. Unfortunately for one member of the band, his indulgence became an inhibitor to his freedom.

Adam Clayton, the bassist and only non-Christian in the band, reveled in the rock-star lifestyle. The other three band members also led the life of rock stars, but Clayton became enslaved to the pitfalls that life offered.

After a breakup with supermodel Naomi Campbell on the Zoo TV tour (1992–93), Clayton turned to alcohol to assuage his grief. His form of self-medication caused him to miss a U2 performance and eventually revealed to him the depth of his dependence upon alcohol. It was this seemingly devastating event that offered him his first foray into freedom.

Paul's one caution to the believers at Galatia was that they not use their freedom to indulge their sinful nature. Because just as legalism could easily make one a slave, the sinful nature could be just as enslaving.

> "I don't like to abuse alcohol–anything you abuse will abuse you back."
> – Bono[6]

After Clayton's missed performance, he began to evaluate the lifestyle to which he had become enslaved. His evaluation led to his sobriety. In an interview with the *The Montreal Gazette* in 2001, Clayton described his decision to quit drinking, stating that it,

> kind of brought be me back down to earth, and now, having gone through all that, I definitely prefer it the way it is. I feel much more focused, much more . . . useful.[7]

Sounds as though he felt much more free too.

In Galatians 5:13, Paul's warning regarding the sinful nature was accompanied by a precautionary commandment. Instead of indulging the sinful nature, Paul challenged them to serve one another in love. Perhaps Paul knew it would be difficult to become enslaved to one's own desires when one focused on the desires of others.

Paul expounds on his commandment in Galatians 5:14. What does he say regarding the law?

____

____

____

Love seems to be the operative word in this passage. Loving others as you love yourself keeps believers from being enslaved to both inhibitors of freedom: legalism and the flesh. Since legalism is rooted in judgment and criticism, it's difficult to be legalistic when you're filled with love for others. Likewise, it's also challenging to

6. Assaya, 23.
7. Mark LePage, "Bass Notes: U2's Adam Clayton on Geography, Spirituality and Rock 'n' Roll," *The Montreal Gazette*, May 26, 2001.

yield to the slavery of self-gratification when you're filled with love for yourself. Because true love for self is not overindulgent; it's self-controlled, but not self-condemning. Love for self causes us to respect ourselves, to see our potential for good, and to accept ourselves, even though we've not yet achieved that potential.

Love is the great equalizer. It keeps us from judging others. It keeps us from overindulgence. It keeps us from self-hatred and self-loathing. And most of all, it keeps us free.

Consider your freedom. How is your freedom evidenced through your love for others and your love for yourself?

Prayer–*Father, I think my freedom is evidenced by my love for others who are not like me–others who may or may not know you and others whose faith walk does not mirror mine. I also think your freedom for me is revealed in a greater love for myself. When I'm enslaved to legalism, I don't allow myself to fail or make mistakes. Of course I do fail and make mistakes, but I beat myself up because of it. But when I truly love myself as you intend for me to, I'm not as hard on myself. I realize that it's okay to mess up and fail, and it is then that I realize–I am truly free.*

Day 5: Freedom

Read Galatians 5:16–26.

According to Galatians 5:16, if we live by the Spirit, what will happen?

According to Galatians 5:18, if the Spirit leads us, what are we free from?

I think it was very thoughtful of Paul to let us know how very liberating the Spirit can be. Through these two verses in Galatians, Paul informs readers that a life led by the Spirit is liberated from both the flesh and the law. But no matter how much I study this text, I cannot find out *how* you live by the Spirit. Oh, what I would give to have a detailed description of *how* to live by the Spirit–perhaps a manual entitled *The Idiot's Guide to Living by the Spirit.* But the closest "how-to-manual" we get is verses 22 and 23, which give us the proof of a life lived by the Spirit.

According to these verses, what does a life lived by the Spirit produce?

In the book *Bono: In Conversation*, published in 2005, Bono speaks to music journalist Michka Assaya about fellow band member, Adam Clayton. When asked if every member of the band was a believer, Bono answered,

> Yes, Adam had his own path, and it took him further out into the world. But I would say Adam is, right now, the most spiritually centered of the band . . . I think he is the person who is now the most watchful of the sheep as they stray out of the herd.[8]

In John 10, Christ compares himself to a shepherd and his followers to sheep. Read John 10:2–4. What do the sheep do in this passage?

____

____

____

To me, living by the Spirit means we listen to and follow the voice of our Shepherd. I think Adam Clayton knew what it felt like to live outside the bounds of the Shepherd's voice. His time spent outside the herd has made him all the more protective of the sheep that stray.

We are all sheep. Some may be attempting to live life outside the herd, by indulging the sinful nature or by striving for self-righteousness. But hopefully, most of us are attempting to live a Spirit-led life. Such a life is spent following the Shepherd's voice, and is evidenced by love, joy, peace, and the other attributes of the fruit of the Spirit. It is a difficult life to navigate, mainly because it requires us to follow a voice that is often varied in its delivery. For example, sometimes our Shepherd speaks through his Word. Sometimes he speaks direct-

8. Assaya, 64.

ly to our hearts. Other times he uses others to speak truth to us. And sometimes, he remains quiet and we must follow him by faith.

Unfortunately, there is no guidebook available for believers to learn the six steps to a Spirit-led life, no instruction manual to ensure us a successful walk with the Spirit. Therefore, we are required to follow blindly, never fully sure of where we are going, only confident of one thing–the one who calls us also goes before us (see John 10:4).

And this walk of faith is what liberates us from the legalistic crutches of rules and regulations. It's also what guides us through the pitfalls of our own destructive sinful nature. And it is the one thing that allows us to experience true freedom.

What has the Shepherd's voice spoken to you lately?

Prayer–*Lord, I'm not going to lie to you; my life would be much easier if you gave me a set of instructions for the Spirit-led life. But if you did that, then we both know I would become dependent upon my own ability to follow your instructions instead of becoming dependent upon you. The Spirit-led life is not an easy life, but it is truly freeing to know that I can know and hear your voice. I may not always get things the first time, but if it's really important to you, you always make your point clear. And for that, I am thankful. So please, Lord, give me the faith to keep walking.*

BREAKAWAY TO LOVE

Galatians Chapter 6

VOW: "Therefore, as we have opportunity, let us do good to all people, especially to those who belong to the family of believers."	**Galatians 6:10**

Day 1: Apartheid

Read Galatians 6:1, 2.

In the West Germanic "Afrikaans" language, which is spoken primarily in South Africa, the word, "apartheid" means "separateness" or "apart-ness." Instituted in South Africa by the all-white National Party in 1948, the policy of apartheid was to separate the racial groups in South Africa both physically and politically, with the eventual goal being a complete separation of blacks and whites.

This socially unjust system of apartheid created animosity between fellow countrymen. During the years it existed, it produced much bloodshed and hatred. Had South Africans been waging war against an invading country, such bloodshed may have been warranted, but because the war they waged was against themselves, their bloodshed was a greater tragedy.

Read Galatians 5:15. What is Paul's warning in this verse?

Like South Africans of the mid-to-late twentieth century, we Christians are just as prone to wage a war against ourselves. In the two final chapters of Galatians, Paul issues advice for Christians to keep them from warring against their fellow believers. He presents several directives throughout chapter five, and he ends that chapter with the admonition for Christians to avoid being conceited and to avoid provoking and envying each other (Galatians 5:26).

His next command to avoid warfare is given in Galatians 6:1. What is it?

Perhaps the greatest lesson to be learned in this verse is not necessarily what Paul says, but rather what he does not say. Let me explain.

During the 1980s, apartheid still held the country of South Africa firmly within its grasp. Despite numerous revolts by the black community and reprimands from the United Nations, the white government continued to oppress and discriminate against the majority of its citizens. In order to maintain their dictatorial rule over the black population, the government ordered all white South African males to enlist in the military. This law resulted in the exodus of many white males, who fled the country to avoid enlistment.

One such person fled the country during the mid 1980s and

eventually settled in the small town of Charlottesville, Virginia. At the age of nineteen, David John Matthews, who would later become the front man for the Dave Matthews Band, found that the greatest role he could play in the war against apartheid was not to participate in the advancement of the apartheid regime. Matthews fought the enemy of apartheid by refusing to be a willing participant in it.

Apartheid separated and segregated South Africans. Sin in the body of Christ also causes separation and segregation. To make matters worse, sin in the life of a Christian often elicits condemnation from other believers. Therefore, when believers condemn each other, we become the catalyst by which sin and segregation are further advanced. Just as Matthews avoided enlistment in an army created to advance the division between his fellow countrymen, we too should avoid enlistment in the army of condemnation, which exists solely to advance the division between fellow believers.

Paul's directive in Galatians 6:1 challenges Christians to refrain from participating in pride and judgment. In essence, he tells them not to err on the side of apartheid. Rather, we are to fight apartheid by refusing to judge and condemn other believers for their sins. He plainly instructs Christians not only to avoid condemning fallen believers but also to attempt to restore them.

According to verse 1, how are we to restore them?

____

____

____

Why does Paul caution us to "watch" ourselves?

____

____

Both gentleness and humility are important in the process of restoring another believer. They benefit the fallen believer, but they also serve to protect us from the pitfall of judgment and condemnation. It is difficult to judge and condemn when we are keenly aware of our own propensity to fall prey to sin.

What does Paul instruct us to do in Galatians 6:2?

___

___

___

According to the book *The Dave Matthews Band: Step Into the Light*, Dave Matthews

> participated in protest marches to end apartheid . . . and he also experienced overwhelming feelings of helplessness, because he knew that the rest of the world was unaware of the level of atrocity occurring daily in the streets of Johannesburg.[1]

Dave Matthews was a white man in a country dominated by a white government. He had no reason to grieve over his status in life. But grieve he did, not over his own life, but over the lives of his persecuted countrymen. His actions model for us the actions of a burden-bearer.

Galatians 6:2 is a challenge to Christians to be burden-bearers and not apartheid-advancers. Dave Matthews recognized apartheid as his country's greatest threat. It threatened to divide them and destroy them. As burden-bearers, we too should recognize sin in the body as our greatest threat, doing whatever we can to keep it from

1. Morgan Delancey, *The Dave Matthews Band: Step Into the Light* (Toronto Ontario: ECW Press, 2001), 19.

dividing and destroying members of the faith. And according to Paul, the best way to assist those who have fallen beneath the weight of sin is to walk beside them, bearing their burden as they walk the path of restoration.

According to 1 Peter 4:8, what attribute allows us to walk beside those who have sinned?

Answer the following questions if applicable:

Cite a time you showed love and mercy to another believer who had fallen into sin.

Was there a time you were shown love and mercy by another believer when you had fallen prey to sin? If so, how did this believer's actions make you feel?

April 27th is a national holiday in South Africa. It is known as "Freedom Day," and it is celebrated annually to commemorate the day in 1994 when South Africans were completely liberated from the apartheid era. And in a sense, it also represents the day they were given full permission to unite and bear each other's burdens.

Prayer–*Lord, thank you for the freedom to unite and bear my neighbor's burdens. Thank you that when we become burden-bearers instead of apartheid-advancers, sin need no longer separate us from our brothers and sisters in Christ. Thank you for such a liberating love. May I love others despite their sin, and in turn, may I too be loved despite my sin.*

Day 2: The Standard of Comparison

Read Galatians 6:3–5.

Under the policy of apartheid, sections of South Africa were divided up in order to house the various races, with 87 percent of the land allocated for whites, coloreds, and Indians. The remaining 13 percent of the country was allotted to the black population, which comprised 60 percent of the overall population of South Africa. Citizens of each territory were only allowed to vote within their racially segregated homelands. Through this process, the white South Africans, who held the majority of the political power in the country, hoped to rid themselves of the black population by encouraging them to form their own, independent homelands.

Why do you think the white South Africans were so intent on ridding themselves of the black population?

I think the white politicians of South Africa viewed the black citizens of their country as a threat, and therefore, they oppressed them. Pride is often the motivating force behind oppression, while fear and intimidation are the motivating forces behind pride. Prideful people are fearful people who live life threatened by their neighbor.

In Galatians 6:3, Paul describes the thought process of a prideful person. What is that thought process, and what does Paul say this person is doing to himself?

One way a prideful person attempts to eliminate his fear and intimidation is by convincing himself that he is better than he really is. But according to Paul, this form of self-medication is really deceitful, primarily because in order to feel good about himself, he must first compare himself to his neighbor. This method of comparison was never God's intent.

Read 2 Corinthians 10:12. How does Paul describe people who compare themselves to others?

Read Galatians 6:4, 5. Instead of comparing ourselves to others, what should we do?

Today, as a unified country, South Africans can look back upon their history with pride. By recognizing their ability to overcome the internal threat of apartheid, South Africans possess an incredible testimony of resilience for the rest of the world. Likewise, each Christian possesses some form of testimony, some witness to the change God has produced in his or her own life.

God desires for us to compare ourselves to our old selves so he can boast of the change he has accomplished in our lives. Independent of our neighbor's spiritual progress, our spiritual standard of comparison is the life we once lived before Christ changed us.

Evaluate your testimony. What changes has God brought about in your life? What bondages were you once enslaved to that you are now free from?

Whatever our answer is to the above question, therein should our security lie. Fear and intimidation need no longer convince us that we are better (or worse) than our neighbor, because according to Galatians 6:5, we are to each bear our own burden. This does not mean we are not to bear each other's burden (Galatians 6:2). What it means is that we each must realize our own accountability to God. We are responsible for our own walk with the Lord, independent of our neighbor's.

When we realize God does not evaluate us based on our neighbor's spiritual progress, it makes the commandment to love our neighbor a little easier. We're not in competition with our neighbor. We're not expected to perform to his or her level of spiritual maturity. When we truly embrace this belief, our neighbor is no longer a threat. Our pride abates because our fears and intimidations are set aside. And we are given opportunity to celebrate Freedom Day with the South Africans, because we too are free to love our neighbor.

Prayer—*Oh God, I've always compared myself to others. I can't stand it, and yet I do it. Thank you for allowing me to understand that your standard of comparison is not at all like my standard of comparison. You do not compare me to others, so please; give me the courage to stop doing that myself, because it hinders my ability to truly love my neighbor.*

Day 3: Sowing for Reasons of Love

Read Galatians 6:6–10.

Not many people know Vusi Mahlasela, unless they're from South Africa. For in South Africa, he is known as "The Voice." He earned this title as a black musician whose attempts to advance the cause of freedom in his country during the apartheid era came in the form of song. As a teenager in South Africa, Dave Matthews was deeply influenced by the music of Mahlasela–so much so that in 1997, Matthews made a promise to Mahlasela that the two would one day record a song together.[2]

Read Galatians 6:6. What does Paul instruct recipients of the Word to do?

____

____

____

After that, Paul inserts a few verses having to do with sowing and reaping. What does he say in these verses (Galatians 6:7, 8)?

____

____

What do these verses have to do with Galatians 6:6?

____

____

In 2001, the Dave Matthews Band released the hit album *Everyday*. On the title track, "Everyday," Matthews enlisted the participation of the man who had inspired him during his teen years in South Africa. Fulfilling the promise he had made to Mahlasela years before, Matthews asked Mahlasela to contribute vocals to the upbeat song, which talks about spreading love to others on a daily basis.

Not long after that, Matthews signed Mahlasela to his own

2. Ibid, 246.

record label, ATO Records, in hopes of catapulting Mahlasela's music beyond the borders of South Africa. By releasing the album *The Voice* in 2003, in which Mahlasela sings his anthems in six different languages, both Matthews and Mahlasela have made his music more accessible to the rest of the world.

In some ways, Mahlasela sowed into the life of Dave Matthews during the apartheid era. Years later, having attained a notable level of success himself, Matthews took the opportunity to sow into the life of Mahlasela. Similarly, in today's passage, Paul challenges everyone, regardless of whether they are students or instructors, to sow into the lives of others.

In Galatians 6:7, 8, Paul instructs believers to sow to please the Spirit instead of sowing to pleasing the flesh. Since each believer possesses the Spirit within, Paul is encouraging us not only to cultivate the Spirit that resides within us individually, but also that same Spirit residing within the lives of other believers. So that when we do invest lovingly into the lives of others, we are in actuality sowing to please the Spirit. Instead of sowing selfishly to please our own wants and desires, we are cultivating something more more eternal–the Spirit.

What does Galatians 6:9 say?

____

____

What does Paul tell us to do in Galatians 6:10?

____

____

____

Sowing into the lives of others can be a rather arduous task, often marked with discouragement and despair. But if we refuse to quit, we will eventually reap a harvest. And as we await the harvest, Paul encourages us to continue to do good to others, especially believers. His directive to do good causes me to wonder how we can actually sow into other people's lives. Paul certainly sowed into the Galatians' lives. First he brought them the greatest truth in the world–the gospel. Next he sowed love and correction when he rebuked them in the first part of Galatians for having believed the lies of the Judaizers. Then he sowed words of encouragement and instruction, teaching them to love each other and encouraging them to sow into each other's lives by doing good.

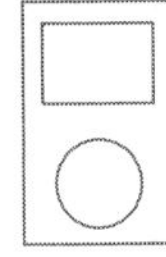

Interact with Your iPod®

Download the song "Everyday" from the Dave Matthew's Band hit album *Everyday.*

- According to this song, what is it we need for everyday?
- In this song, what is love capable of doing?

What do you think motivated Paul to sow into the lives of others?

I think the word that is constantly repeated in the song "Everyday" is exactly what motivated Paul to sow into the lives of others. I think it was love. Love was the motivating force behind Paul's passionate letter to the Galatians. Love was the motivation for his rebuke of them. And love was the reason he encouraged them to love each other, because he knew the life-changing effects love could render. Love was what Paul knew the Galatians needed. Because, as the Dave Matthews Band claims, love has the ability to pick you up and place you on top.

Think of the people who have lovingly sown into your spiritual life. Below, write a note of gratitude to one of these people.

Prayer—*Lord, thank you for the people in my life who have sown your seeds of love. My life is the richer for their endeavors, and may they never think their efforts on my behalf were in vain. May you bless each of them, Father, and may my life reflect their harvest.*

Day 4: Tainted Love

Read Galatians 6:11–14.

What does Paul tell his audience in Galatians 6:11?

After offering the Galatian Christians both rebuke and encouragement, Paul draws his letter to a close. Today, as we study a portion of his final thoughts, it's important to observe the urgency found in Paul's statement to the Galatians in verse 11. Scholars have varying opinions regarding the meaning of this scripture. One theory is that Paul had dictated earlier portions of his letter to another person but opted to write the closing section himself to give the letter authenticity. Some have speculated that Paul was suffering poor vision at this time and had to write large enough so that he could see his own words. Still others believe his mention of large letters could mean that he was adding emphasis to this final section.

Study Galatians 6:12, 13. Why do you think Paul would emphasize these verses?

____

____

____

No one could have anticipated the atrocities that occurred in America on September 11, 2001. As the world watched in stunned horror, thousands lost their lives to a group of merciless terrorists intent on striking fear into the heart of every American. Unfortunately, their surprise attack did cause Americans, who were previously accustomed to peace, protection, and freedom, to begin to fear.

According to Galatians 6:12, why did the Judaizers want the Galatians to be circumcised?

____

____

____

Fear can be a powerful motivator. It motivated our country for months after the 9/11 attacks, causing a decline in air travel and an increase in sales for items such as duct tape, gas masks, and any type of survival gear capable of protecting people against the threat of biological warfare.

According to Paul, fear also motivated the Judaizers. Their fear, which caused them to impose the law of circumcision upon the Galatians, stemmed from their dread of being persecuted. But fear was not their only motivation.

Read Galatians 6:13. What was another reason the Judaizers wanted the Galatians to be circumcised?

____

____

The Judaizers taught a message rooted in fear because they themselves were motivated by fear. But fear was not their only motivating force. Their desire to boast about the Galatians reveals that pride and selfishness were also key motivators. Perhaps Paul wrote these final statements in large letters because he wanted the Galatians to know the truth about the Judaizers. He wanted them to know the true motives behind their actions.

Galatians 6:14 reveals Paul's motives for ministry. In what does he boast?

____

____

A week and a half after 9/11, *MTV News* released an article about musicians who were reconsidering their music in light of the attacks. One such musician was Dave Matthews, whose band had planned to release, as a radio single, the song "When the World Ends" from their

Everyday album. According to the band's publicist, Dave "changed his mind about releasing 'When the World Ends' as his band's next radio single, feeling it would be insensitive given people's fears after the deadly hijackings."[3] Instead of "When the World Ends," Dave Matthews opted to release the song, "Everyday" as a radio single. "Everyday," which talks about spreading love to others, was much more appropriate in the aftermath of the terrorist attacks.

Love, true love, never preys upon the fears of others. Nor is it motivated by fear, pride, or selfishness. The Galatians may have thought the Judaizers deeply cared for them and even loved them. But in verse 14, Paul reveals to the Galatians what true love is, or rather, what it is not. True love is not boastful or selfish; it does not exploit the object of its affection. It does not impose fear upon others, nor does it manipulate others by fear. Love's only reason for boasting is found in the cross of Jesus Christ, the ultimate symbol of love.

The Galatians were duped by the Judaizers into believing they were truly loved, when in actuality, the love they were given was tainted with selfishness, fear, and pride. Have you ever been in a relationship where love was tainted in one or more of these ways? How did it make you feel?

____

____

____

____

____

____

3. Eric Schumacher-Rasmussen, "Dave Matthews Band, Strokes, Sheryl Crow Rethink Their Music," *MTV News*, September 21, 2001, http://www.vh1.com/news/articles/1449031/09212001/dave_matthews_band.jhtml.

Unfortunately, because we are imperfect people, we are all capable of falling prey to relationships based upon tainted love. We're capable of receiving a tainted love from others, and we're also capable of offering a tainted love to others. But the more we encounter the love of Christ and the more we understand the love he lavishes upon us, the more capable we will be of recognizing a pure, sincere love when we experience it. And best of all, as a result of Christ's love, we will be more capable of producing a pure love.

Prayer—*Father, thank you for your limitless love for me. Thank you that your love is pure and sincere, unhindered by selfishness, fear, and pride. Teach me more about this love so that it may be reproduced through me.*

Day 5: A New Creation

Read Galatians 6:15–18.

While living in Charlottesville, Virginia, in the early 1990s, Dave Matthews began acting in several local plays. He demonstrated talent as a young actor, but his passion for music delayed his theatrical career. However, in 2005, after more than a decade away from the stage, Matthews returned to acting in the heartwarming movie *Because of Winn Dixie.*

By playing a mysterious pet shop worker whose dialogue with others is more sung than spoken, Matthews treats audiences to his musical talents. During one scene with leading actress AnnaSophia Robb, Matthews' character sings a song to Robb's character. The song "Butterfly," which is an original song by Matthews, compares the young girl to a butterfly. Through it, he encourages her to metaphorically undergo the transformation from a caterpillar to a butterfly and then go ahead and do what she was created to do–fly.

According to Galatians 6:15, what is truly important?

____

____

____

In this final week of our Galatians study we've examined the concept of true love. In Day One, we discussed love's ability to span the divide of sin created among believers. In Day Two, we learned that when we cease to compare ourselves with others, we're endowed with a greater capacity to love others. Next, in Day Three, we discovered how the motivating force of love causes us to sow good things into others' lives. And in Day Four, we were given the attributes of true love. Here in Day Five, our final day of study together, we will discover what true love produces.

Just as the caterpillar in Matthews' song was destined for greater things, so we too, as believers, are destined for greater things. All we need is the ability to change. If we've learned anything through this study of Galatians, my earnest prayer is that we've recognized our inability to recreate ourselves. Although we need to be transformed, we can never force ourselves into the mold of a "new creation."

According to 2 Corinthians 5:17, how are we transformed into a new creation?

____

____

Only the Lord's grace and love can fashion us into the new creation we're destined to become. Second Corinthians 5:17 tells us that if we are in Christ, then we are a new creation. God's incredible love for us, demonstrated through his Son, Jesus Christ, brings about change in our lives and fashions us into new creations. Each of us is God's new creation. Whether we feel like it or not, we are the product of God's love. We are his new creation in Christ.

Because the Galatian Christians were believers in Christ, they too were a new creation. However, when Paul wrote his letter to them, they weren't acting as such. In fact, they were striving to become a new creation, oblivious to the fact that God had already accomplished this. Paul wrote Galatians to inform them of who they truly were in Christ and to encourage them to walk in the freedom afforded a new creation.

Scientists say caterpillars undergo a complete reformation of their bodily organs while inside their cocoons. In fact, their body mass becomes a soupy liquid during their metamorphosis. But at the end of this miraculous process, they are transformed into a beautiful butterfly. Once they have undergone their changes, they are then required to force their way out of the safe haven they've created for themselves, using their newly formed wings to break free. But once they accomplish their breakaway, they are truly free to do what they were created to do–fly.

The apostle Paul was a new creation. According to Galatians 6:17, what did Paul bear on his body?

____

____

Most scholars believe Paul is referring to the physical scars he had acquired as a result of the persecution he suffered for following Christ. Paul's scars bore evidence of the fact that he, a former Pharisee who once persecuted Christians, was transformed into a new creation and was now among the persecuted. In spite of Paul's infirmities, he took joy in the fact that he was a new creation who had experienced a breakaway from legalism and tradition and had the courage to live life as a new creation.

This past summer, my three small daughters and I engaged in a little science project. We collected some caterpillars in a jar, and after a few days we noticed they had enveloped themselves in their own little cocoons. And thus began our waiting period. We waited and waited for their little bodies to transform into new creations. Unfortunately, we were never given the opportunity to see them as butterflies, because they never came out of their cocoons. They may have undergone the transformation process and actually become butterflies, but because they didn't break free from their cocoons, we never got to see them fly.

God, in his love and mercy, transformed us into a new creation when we accepted the gift of his Son. Transforming us into a new creation is God's gift of love to us. Having the courage to live life as a new creation is our gift of love to God.

I have so many desires for those of you who were inspired to complete this study. I desire for you to realize who you truly are in Christ. I desire for you to accept the fact that you are not in the process of becoming a new creation; you already are one. And that as a new creation, you no longer need focus on your sin (which the law causes us to do), but rather focus on your Savior. Because only Christ can truly set you free.

So go ahead; set your eyes on him and the freedom he offers. Then, break away from the safe haven of legalism and religion and spread your wings and fly–because you were destined to live life as a new creation.

From what you've learned today, answer the following questions:

Who are you?

____

____

____

____

Why is it important that you truly believe that?

____

____

____

Prayer—*Lord, I want to thank you for giving me the time to complete this study. Thank you for granting me the desire to study your Word. Thank you that my hunger for you has changed my life and has inspired me to break away and be all you've created me to be. My prayer is that many others would do the same; for we were all destined to live life in the freedom afforded a new creation.*

PRAYER JOURNAL